DYSPHAGIA COOKBOOK

These tasty and healthy recipes will help you overcome your swallowing problems so you can eat again confidently.

By Andrea Knepp

TABLE OF CONTENTS

CHAPTER 1: DYSPHAGIA (SWALLOWING PROBLEMS) 5
    About dysphagia 5
    Causes of dysphagia 6
    Diagnosing dysphagia 8
    Treating dysphagia 11
        High (oropharyngeal) dysphagia 11
        Low (oesophageal) dysphagia 13
        Surgery 13
        Congenital dysphagia 14
CHAPTER 2: A SAFE WAY TO SWALLOW 16

RECIPES FOR DYSPHAGIA 18

CHAPTER 3: SOFT FOOD RECIPES 18
    Soft And Creamy Scrambled Eggs 18
    Mashed Sweet Potatoes 18
    Cream Of Mushroom Soup 19
    Cottage Cheese With Fruit 20
    Creamy Carrot-Ginger Soup 21
    Creamy Mashed Potato 22
    Easy Creamy Mushroom And Spinach Risotto 23
    Healthy Mashed Sweet Potatoes With Greek Yogurt 25
    Creamy Broccoli Soup 26
    Avocado Egg Salad 27
    Butternut Squash Risotto 27
    Banana Oatmeal 28
    Tropical Fruit Baked Oatmeal 29
    Creamy Chicken And Rice 30
    Cauliflower Purée With Thyme 32
CHAPTER 4: PUREED FOOD RECIPES 33
    Cauliflower Purée With Thyme 33
    Mashed Sweet Potatoes 33
    Broccoli Purée 34
    Chicken, Rice, And Carrot Puree 35
    Homemade Sweet Potato Puree 35
    Apple Puree / Sauce 37
    Classic Pureed Tuna Salad 37
    Pureed Carrot Soup 38
    Turkey Gravy And Garlic Potato Purée 39
    Perfect Banana & Avocado Purée 40
    Chicken & Mixed Veg Purée 41
    Creamy Mushroom Soup 41
    Yogurt And Fruit Purée Breakfast 43
    Carrot-Ginger Puree 43
    Creamy Butternut Squash Soup Recipe 44
    Greek Yoghurt Berry Smoothie 45
CHAPTER 5: LIQUID FOOD RECIPES 46
    Creamy Potato Soup 46
    Strawberry Banana Smoothie 47

Tomato Basil Soup	48
Carrot Ginger Soup	49
Creamy Vegetable Soup	50
Blueberry Smoothie	51
Awesome Broccoli Cheese Soup	51
Broccoli Cheddar Soup	52
Minestrone Soup	53
Easy Blueberry Oatmeal	54
Chicken Noodle Soup	55
Butternut Squash Soup	56
Easy Broccoli Cheese Soup	56
CHAPTER 6: SOLID FOOD RECIPES	**58**
Country Style Gravy Meatballs	58
Turkey Meatloaf	59
Avocado Scrambled Eggs	61
Roasted Vegetable Puree	61
Chicken And Rice Casserole	62
Chicken And Rice Casserole	64
Sweet Potato Black Bean Bowls	65
Beef Stroganoff	67
Honey Glazed Chicken With Sweet Potato Mash	69
Southwest Shredded Chicken Salad	70
Meatballs In Tomato Sauce	71
Ground Beef Stroganoff	72
Meatballs & Mashed Potatoes	73
CHAPTER 7: BEVERAGES RECIPES	**75**
Strawberry Banana Smoothie	75
Chocolate Almond Milk	75
Creamy Vanilla Milkshake	76
Pineapple Coconut Water	77
Apple Cinnamon Smoothie	77
Blueberry Iced Green Tea	78
Vanilla Chai Latte	78
Orange Creamsicle Smoothie	79
Homemade Sports Drink	80
Creamy Coconut Milkshake	80
Carrot Ginger Juice Recipe	81
Creamy Mango Lassi	82
CHAPTER 8: SNACK AND DESSERTS RECIPES	**83**
Banana Oatmeal Cookies	83
Yogurt Parfait	85
Chocolate Avocado Pudding	85
Peanut Butter And Jelly Smoothie	86
Homemade Cinnamon Applesauce	87
Easy Chia Pudding	87
Baked Cinnamon Apple Chips	89
Soft Oatmeal Cookies	90
Easy Poached Pears	91
Healthy Mango Yogurt Smoothie	92
Baked Apple Slices	93

Introduction

We understand that receiving a dysphagia diagnosis can be frightening and frustrating. This book was created to help you navigate the dysphagia journey, starting with the diagnosis and moving on to managing it in your daily life. Because we believe that no one should be forced to go through life without the joy of eating food and drink, we have provided you with 100 recipes, useful information, and beneficial counsel.

Dysphagia is a condition in which a food bolus moves abnormally slowly from the oropharynx to the stomach. Many people typically struggle with swallowing. Dysphagia is a common symptom among persons. However, it is critical to keep in mind that an underlying medical problem often causes dysphagia. Swallowing has three phases: oral (preparatory), pharyngeal (transfer), and esophageal. Dysphagia usually comprises of both pharyngeal and esophageal phases.

CHAPTER 1: DYSPHAGIA (SWALLOWING PROBLEMS)

ABOUT DYSPHAGIA

Swallowing difficulties are referred to as dysphagia in the medical field. Individuals with dysphagia may experience difficulties when trying to consume certain foods or liquids, and in some cases, they may be unable to swallow altogether.

Additional indications of dysphagia include:

- Experiencing difficulty while eating or drinking
- Experiencing regurgitation, occasionally through the nasal passage
- Experiencing a feeling of food being lodged in your throat or chest
- Experiencing excessive saliva drooling

Over time, dysphagia can lead to symptoms like weight loss and recurrent chest infections.

If you're experiencing any issues with swallowing, schedule an appointment with your primary care physician.

What causes dysphagia?

Dysphagia is commonly associated with various health conditions, including those that affect the nervous system, such as stroke, head injury, or dementia, as well as certain types of cancer, like mouth cancer or oesophageal cancer.

Gastro-oesophageal reflux disease (GORD) occurs when stomach acid leaks back into the oesophagus.

It's worth noting that dysphagia can also affect children due to developmental or learning disabilities.

Dysphagia can arise from issues with the mouth or throat, specifically oropharyngeal or 'high' dysphagia.

Difficulty swallowing, also referred to as oesophageal or 'low' dysphagia, affects the tube that transports food from your mouth to your stomach.

Treating dysphagia

The treatment approach typically varies based on the underlying cause and specific type of dysphagia. Typically, the diagnosis of your dysphagia can be determined by assessing your swallowing function and conducting an examination of your oesophagus.

Treatment can often improve many cases of dysphagia, although a complete cure may not always be achievable. There are various treatments for this type of dysphagia:

- Speech and language therapy can help you acquire new techniques for swallowing. Modifying the texture of food and liquids to enhance their safety for swallowing
- Other options for feeding, like using a tube to deliver nutrients through the nose or stomach
- A procedure can be performed to address the narrowing of the oesophagus by either stretching it or inserting a stent made of plastic or metal.

Complications of dysphagia

Difficulty swallowing can sometimes result in additional complications. A frequent issue that individuals may experience is the occurrence of coughing or choking due to the obstruction of the airway when food is mistakenly swallowed.

If this happens often, you might start avoiding food and drink out of fear of choking, which can result in malnutrition and dehydration.

Individuals who experience dysphagia may be at risk of developing chest infections, including aspiration pneumonia that necessitate professional medical intervention.

Having difficulty swallowing can significantly impact your daily life, making it challenging to fully enjoy meals and social gatherings.

CAUSES OF DYSPHAGIA

Given the intricacies involved in the process of swallowing, there are numerous factors that can contribute to the development of dysphagia.

Neurological causes

The nervous system consists of the brain, nerves, and spinal cord. When the nervous system is affected, it can disrupt the nerves that initiate and regulate the process of swallowing. Dysphagia may be a potential consequence of this.

There are several neurological factors that can contribute to dysphagia:

- Having a stroke can lead to various neurological conditions that gradually affect the brain and nervous system. These conditions may include Parkinson's disease, multiple sclerosis, dementia, and motor neuron disease.
- Brain tumors are a serious medical condition that require specialized attention.

- Myasthenia gravis is a relatively uncommon condition that leads to muscle weakness.

Congenital and developmental conditions

When it comes to certain conditions, they are present from birth. Developmental conditions can have an impact on your overall development.

There are certain conditions that can lead to dysphagia, which are present from birth or develop over time.

- Difficulties with learning, understanding, and communicating
- Cerebral palsy is a collection of neurological conditions that impact movement and coordination.
- A cleft lip and palate is a frequently occurring birth defect that causes a separation or division in the upper lip or roof of the mouth.

Obstruction

Swallowing can become challenging when there is an obstruction in the throat or a narrowing of the oesophagus, which is the tube responsible for carrying food from the mouth to the stomach.

There are several factors that can lead to obstruction and narrowing:

- If mouth cancer or throat cancer, like laryngeal cancer or esophageal cancer, are successfully treated, the obstruction may no longer be a concern.
- A pharyngeal pouch, also called Zenker diverticulum, is a condition where a sac forms in the upper part of the esophagus, causing difficulty in swallowing both liquids and solids. This condition is uncommon and is typically found in older individuals.
- A condition called eosinophilic oesophagitis can occur when certain factors trigger a reaction in the lining of the oesophagus. This reaction leads to the accumulation of a specific type of white blood cell called eosinophil, which in turn damages the lining and causes difficulties with swallowing.
- Radiotherapy treatment may result in the formation of scar tissue, which can lead to a narrowing of the passageway in your throat and oesophagus. Gastro-oesophageal reflux disease (GORD) can also cause scar tissue to develop, leading to a narrowing of the oesophagus due to stomach acid. Infections such as tuberculosis or thrush can cause inflammation of the oesophagus (oesophagitis).

Muscular conditions

It is uncommon for dysphagia to occur as a result of conditions that affect the muscles responsible for pushing food down the oesophagus and into the stomach.

There are two muscular conditions that can be associated with dysphagia:

- Scleroderma is a condition in which the immune system mistakenly targets healthy tissue, causing stiffness in the muscles of the throat and esophagus.
- Achalasia is a condition in which the muscles in the esophagus lose their ability to relax and open, making it difficult for food or liquid to enter the stomach.

Other causes

As individuals age, the muscles responsible for swallowing may experience a decline in strength. It's not uncommon for dysphagia to be more prevalent among the elderly population. There are effective treatments available for individuals experiencing age-related dysphagia.

Chronic obstructive pulmonary disease (COPD) encompasses a range of lung conditions that can significantly impair proper breathing. Difficulty with swallowing can occasionally be a result of respiratory issues.

Occasionally, dysphagia may arise as a result of head or neck surgery.

DIAGNOSING DYSPHAGIA

If you're experiencing any trouble with swallowing, it's important to consult your general practitioner. A thorough evaluation will be conducted, followed by potential recommendations for additional examinations and therapies.

Tests can be conducted to determine the cause of your dysphagia, whether it originates from your mouth or throat (oropharyngeal, or 'high' dysphagia), or from your oesophagus, the tube that transports food from the mouth to the stomach (oesophageal, or 'low' dysphagia).

Accurate diagnosis of the type of dysphagia can greatly enhance the effectiveness of treatment and minimize the risk of complications, such as choking or pneumonia.

Your doctor will want to know:

- May I inquire about the duration of your dysphagia?
- Whether your symptoms fluctuate or are becoming more severe
- Have you experienced any difficulties with swallowing solid foods, liquids, or both? Additionally, have you noticed any changes in your weight?

Specialist referral

Based on the potential cause, additional tests may be recommended:

- a doctor who specializes in treating conditions related to the ear, nose, and throat (ENT)
- a professional who specializes in speech and language therapy
- A neurologist is an expert in diagnosing and treating conditions that impact the brain, nerves, and spinal cord.
- A gastroenterologist is a highly skilled doctor who focuses on diagnosing and treating various conditions that affect the gullet, stomach, and intestines.
- An expert in the field of geriatric care, focusing on the well-being of older individuals.

Water swallow test

A water swallow test is typically conducted by a speech and language therapist, providing a valuable initial assessment of your swallowing abilities. You will be provided with 150ml of water and instructed to consume it as rapidly as you can.

We will keep track of the duration it takes for you to consume the water and the total number of sips needed. You may also be requested to consume a soft piece of pudding or fruit.

Video fluoroscopy

An expert in the field can utilize a video fluoroscopy, also known as a modified barium swallow, to accurately evaluate your swallowing function and pinpoint the specific issue.

A specialized medical professional can utilize an X-ray machine to capture a dynamic video of your swallowing process, enabling a thorough examination of your swallowing difficulties.

You will be requested to ingest various types of food and beverages with different textures, combined with a harmless liquid known as barium that is visible on X-rays.

The duration of a videofluoroscopy is typically around 30 minutes. It is possible to experience some discomfort following the test, and the barium may lead to constipation. It is possible for your stools to appear white for a few days as the barium moves through your body.

Nasoendoscopy

An nasendoscopy, also referred to as fibreoptic endoscopic evaluation of swallowing (FEES), is a procedure that involves the use of a small flexible tube called an endoscope to closely examine the nose and upper airways.

An endoscope is gently inserted into your nasal passage, allowing the expert to observe your throat and upper airways. There is a device with a light and camera that allows for viewing of throat images on a television screen. This enables the identification of any blockages or problem areas.

Testing for oropharyngeal dysphagia typically involves swallowing a small amount of test liquid, such as colored water or milk, during a FEES procedure.

Prior to the procedure, a local anesthetic spray may be applied to your nose. This helps to minimize any discomfort, and it is important to note that the camera used in the procedure does not extend into your throat, so there is no need to worry about experiencing retching. The procedure is generally considered safe and typically only requires a few minutes of your time.

Manometry and 24-hour pH study

Manometry is a procedure that helps evaluate the performance of your oesophagus. A small tube with pressure sensors is inserted through your nose and into your esophagus to monitor its function.

This test assesses the pressures in your oesophagus during swallowing to evaluate its functionality.

The 24-hour pH study requires the insertion of a tube into the oesophagus through the nose to measure the reflux of stomach acid. This can assist in identifying the underlying factors contributing to any challenges with swallowing.

Diagnostic gastroscopy

Manometry is a procedure that evaluates the functionality of your esophagus. A small tube with pressure sensors is inserted through your nose and into your esophagus to monitor its function.

This test assesses the pressures in your oesophagus during swallowing to evaluate its functionality.

A 24-hour pH study requires the insertion of a tube into the oesophagus through the nose to measure the acid reflux from the stomach. This can assist in identifying the underlying factors contributing to any issues with swallowing.

Nutritional assessment

If you're experiencing difficulties with eating due to dysphagia, it might be necessary to undergo a nutritional assessment to ensure that you're receiving adequate nutrients and to address any potential malnourishment. Some possible aspects to consider could include:

Assessing your body weight

Assessing your body mass index (BMI) to determine if your weight is within a healthy range for your height. Conducting blood tests to gather necessary information.

TREATING DYSPHAGIA

There are various treatment options available for swallowing problems tailored to the specific type of dysphagia you are experiencing.

The appropriate treatment for your swallowing problem will be determined by the location of the issue - whether it is in the mouth or throat (oropharyngeal, or 'high' dysphagia), or in the oesophagus (oesophageal, or 'low' dysphagia).

When determining the appropriate treatment, the cause of dysphagia is taken into consideration. In certain situations, addressing the root cause, such as mouth cancer or esophageal cancer, may alleviate difficulties with swallowing.

Treatment for dysphagia can be effectively managed by a team of medical professionals who specialize in different areas and work together to provide comprehensive care. A team of experts, including a speech and language therapist (SLT), a surgeon, and a dietitian, may be part of your medical team.

HIGH (OROPHARYNGEAL) DYSPHAGIA

High dysphagia refers to difficulties in swallowing that arise from issues with the mouth or throat.

Treating the condition can pose a challenge when it is caused by a disorder that impacts the nervous system. This is because these issues typically cannot be resolved through the use of medication or surgical procedures.

There are three primary treatments available for high dysphagia:

- swallowing therapy
- dietary changes
- feeding tubes

Swallowing therapy

If you have high dysphagia, you may be referred to a speech and language therapist (SLT) for swallowing therapy.

A Speech and Language Therapist is a healthcare professional who specializes in assisting individuals with challenges related to feeding or swallowing.

Our team of experts is skilled in utilizing various techniques to address your specific concerns, including providing guidance on specialized exercises to improve your swallowing.

Dietary changes

You may be referred to a nutrition expert for advice about changes to your diet to ensure you receive a healthy, balanced diet.

A speech and language therapist can provide guidance on dietary modifications, such as softer foods and thickened fluids that may be more manageable for swallowing. They may also make efforts to ensure you receive the necessary assistance during meal times.

Feeding tubes

During the recovery process, feeding tubes can be utilized to supply the necessary nutrition until the ability to swallow is regained. In more serious instances of dysphagia, they may be necessary to address the potential dangers of malnutrition and dehydration.

A feeding tube can also facilitate the administration of necessary medication for other conditions.

There are 2 types of feeding tubes:

- a tube is inserted through your nose and into your stomach, known as a nasogastric tube
- A percutaneous endoscopic gastrostomy (PEG) tube is a tube that is inserted directly into the stomach.

Nasogastric tubes are typically intended for temporary use. The tube will need to be replaced and switched to the other nostril after approximately one month. PEG tubes are specifically designed to be used for an extended period of time, typically lasting several months before requiring replacement.

Many individuals with dysphagia find the PEG tube to be a convenient option as it can be discreetly concealed under clothing. Nevertheless, there is a higher likelihood of complications associated with nasogastric tubes.

Common issues with PEG tubes may include the tube shifting, potential skin infections, and problems with blockage or leakage. There are two significant complications that can arise from PEG tubes: infection and internal bleeding.

Adjusting to resuming normal feeding can pose challenges when using a PEG tube as opposed to a nasogastric tube. Using PEG tubes may lead to a decreased motivation for individuals to engage in swallowing exercises and make dietary adjustments, compared to those who rely on nasogastric tubes.

It's important to have a thorough discussion with your treatment team about the advantages and disadvantages of both types of feeding tubes.

LOW (OESOPHAGEAL) DYSPHAGIA

Swallowing difficulties caused by issues with the oesophagus are known as low dysphagia.

Medication

Depending on the underlying cause of low dysphagia, it may be possible to address it through the use of medication. As an expert in the field, it is worth noting that the use of proton pump inhibitors (PPIs) for indigestion can potentially alleviate symptoms associated with the narrowing or scarring of the oesophagus.

Botulinum toxin

Achalasia can sometimes be treated with botulinum toxin. This condition occurs when the muscles in the oesophagus become rigid, making it difficult for food and liquid to pass into the stomach.

It is effective in relaxing the contracted muscles that hinder the passage of food to the stomach. However, the duration of the effects is typically limited to approximately 6 months.

SURGERY

Other cases of low dysphagia can usually be treated with surgery.

Endoscopic dilatation

Endoscopic dilation is a commonly employed procedure for addressing dysphagia resulting from blockages. Additionally, it can be utilized to expand your oesophagus in case of scarring.

An endoscopic dilatation procedure will be performed as part of an internal examination of your oesophagus. This will be done using an endoscopy.

A specialized procedure involves inserting an endoscope through your throat and into your oesophagus, allowing for the transmission of internal images to a television screen.

Based on the image provided, a medical procedure involves the insertion of a small balloon or a bougie, a flexible instrument, into the narrowed section of your oesophagus to expand it. If a balloon is utilized, it will be gently inflated to expand your oesophagus before being deflated and extracted.

You may be provided with a mild sedative prior to the procedure to help you relax. There is a slight possibility that the procedure may result in a tear or perforation of your esophagus.

Inserting a stent

If you are diagnosed with inoperable oesophageal cancer, it is typically advised to opt for a stent insertion rather than endoscopic dilatation. This is because, if you have cancer, there is a greater chance of your esophagus being perforated if it is stretched.

A stent, typically a metal mesh tube, is placed into the oesophagus either through an endoscopy procedure or with the assistance of X-ray guidance.

The stent gradually expands to create a passage wide enough for food to pass through. It is important to adhere to a specific dietary plan in order to maintain the openness of the stent and prevent blockages.

CONGENITAL DYSPHAGIA

If your baby has difficulty swallowing from birth, their treatment will depend on the underlying cause.

Cerebral palsy

Speech and language therapy can effectively treat dysphagia caused by cerebral palsy. Your child will receive guidance on swallowing techniques, dietary adjustments, and the utilization of feeding tubes.

Cleft lip and palate

Facial birth defects like cleft lip and palate can lead to difficulties with swallowing, known as dysphagia. Typically, surgery is the recommended course of treatment.

Narrowing of the oesophagus

A potential treatment for narrowing of the oesophagus involves a surgical procedure known as dilatation, which aims to widen the oesophagus.

Gastro-oesophageal reflux disease (GORD)

Special thickened feeds can be used to treat dysphagia caused by gastro-oesophageal reflux disease (GORD), as an alternative to regular breast or formula milk. Occasionally, medication may also be prescribed.

Breastfeeding or bottle feeding

If you're facing challenges with bottle feeding or breastfeeding your baby, it would be beneficial to consult with a midwife, health visitor, or GP.

Complications of dysphagia

One of the primary concerns associated with dysphagia is the occurrence of coughing and choking, which has the potential to result in pneumonia.

Coughing and choking

If you experience dysphagia, there is a potential danger of food, drink, or saliva entering the airway instead of the esophagus. It can obstruct your air passage, leading to breathing difficulties and triggering coughing or choking.

If you experience dysphagia, it is possible to develop a fear of choking as well. However, it is crucial that you do not neglect your food and water intake, as it may lead to dehydration and malnutrition.

If you frequently experience difficulty swallowing due to dysphagia, there is a possibility of developing a condition known as aspiration pneumonia.

Aspiration pneumonia

Aspiration pneumonia is a chest infection that can occur when inhaling foreign substances, such as small pieces of food, by accident. It can lead to irritation or damage in the lungs. Elderly individuals are especially vulnerable to the development of aspiration pneumonia.

Here are some common symptoms of aspiration pneumonia:

Experiencing a cough, whether it's dry or accompanied by phlegm that has varying colors, such as yellow, green, brown, or bloodstained? Noticing a high temperature of 38C (100.4F) or above? Experiencing chest pain?

You may experience difficulty breathing, with rapid and shallow breaths, and a feeling of breathlessness, even when at rest.

Contact your treatment team immediately if you're being treated for dysphagia and you develop these symptoms.

The symptoms of aspiration pneumonia can vary in intensity, and typically, antibiotics are prescribed for treatment. In more serious situations, hospitalization and administration of antibiotics through an IV will be necessary.

In individuals who are particularly elderly or fragile, there is a possibility that the infection may result in the accumulation of fluid in their lungs, hindering their proper functioning. This condition is commonly referred to as acute respiratory distress syndrome (ARDS).

If your immune system is weakened, you have chronic obstructive pulmonary disease (COPD), or if your oral and dental hygiene is poor, your risk of developing pneumonia due to dysphagia increases.

Dysphagia in children

If children experiencing long-term dysphagia do not consume sufficient amounts of food, it can hinder their ability to obtain the necessary nutrients for both physical and mental development.

Children who struggle with eating may also experience stress during meal times, potentially resulting in behavioral issues.

CHAPTER 2: A SAFE WAY TO SWALLOW

Ten Important Suggestions for a Safer Sweeping

1. During meals and drinks, you should maintain an upright stance. When the individual is lying down when eating or drinking, it might be difficult and risky to swallow.
2. After you have finished eating and drinking, you should sit up straight for at least half an hour.
3. When you are eating or drinking, keep distractions to a minimum by, for example, turning off the television or the radio.
4. If you are eating or drinking, refrain from talking.
5. Don't rush through meals; instead, give yourself plenty of time to prepare them.
6. When eating or drinking, take a few nibbles or drinks at a time. Mouthfuls that are too large can be challenging to swallow.
7. Before taking another meal or sip, make sure that you have completely swallowed everything that is currently in your mouth by pausing in between each mouthful.
8. It might be simpler for you to consume smaller meals more frequently if you discover that eating is a demanding activity.
9. Stay away from meals that pose a high risk unless your speech and language therapist specifically instructs you otherwise. Follow all of the recommendations that have been

made by your speech and language therapist or dietitian; these guidelines have been made to ensure that you consume food and drink in a safe manner.
10. It might be simpler for you to consume smaller meals more frequently if you discover that eating is a demanding activity.
11. Family members and caregivers need to ensure the individual is completely awake before providing someone who has difficulty swallowing with food or drink.

DYSPHAGIA'S EFFECTS ON EATING

It's possible that your Speech and Language Therapist would suggest that you try a diet that reduces the amount of food you eat.

This is the point at which your food is modified to make chewing and swallowing in a more comfortable and secure manner.

What Exactly Are Descriptors Of Food?

The level that you require will be recommended on an individual basis by a Speech and Language Therapist after they have evaluated your swallowing ability; therefore, it is of the utmost importance to wait for them to inform you the appropriate level for you on an individual basis.

HIGH RISK FOODS

When it comes to swallowing securely, there are certain meals that are really challenging. These foods should be avoided at all costs unless your Speech and Language Therapist specifically instructs you otherwise. This is not an entire list, so if you have any questions, please let your speech and language therapist know, or if you are unsure, leave it out!

The celery, pineapple, bacon fat, and melted cheese made the dish stringy and fibrous.

Sweetcorn and granary bread contain husks.

Toasted bread, crisps, biscuits, flaky pastry, crumbles, and pie crusts are examples of foods that are crunchy and crumbly.

Durable foods include tough meat, sweets that are chewy and cooked, nuts, and seeds.

Various vegetable and fruit skins, including but not limited to beans, peas, potatoes, orange segments, grapes, and vegetable stalks

Cereals that do not blend with milk, soups that have lumps, and yoghurt that has chunks are examples of meals that have a mixed consistency.

Whipped cream, ice cream, and jelly all turn into a thick liquid when they melt. When it comes to these meals, exercise caution, and only consume them if your Speech and Language Therapist instructs you to do so.

RECIPES FOR DYSPHAGIA

CHAPTER 3: SOFT FOOD RECIPES

SOFT AND CREAMY SCRAMBLED EGGS

PREP 10 MINS COOK 5 MINS TOTAL 15 MINS

Ingredients

- Half a spoonful of butter
- Four big eggs
- 1/8 tsp kosher salt, or more according to preference

Directions

1. Heat the butter in a non-stick pan over medium-low heat.
2. Begin by cracking eggs into a bowl, then add a pinch of salt and whisk until the mixture is well blended.
3. As soon as the butter bubbles, pour the eggs and swiftly swirl them in the pan using a silicone spatula. Keep going in small circles without pausing until the eggs become slightly thickened and tiny curds start to form, which should take around 30 seconds.
4. Switch from creating circular motions to making broad, sweeping movements across the pan until you notice larger, velvety curds forming, approximately 20 seconds.
5. Once the eggs are gently cooked with a slight runniness, take the pan off the heat and let them finish cooking for a few seconds. Make sure to give it a final stir before serving it right away. Enhance the flavors with a touch of salt, a dash of black pepper, and a handful of freshly chopped herbs, if you prefer.

MASHED SWEET POTATOES

PREP TIME: 15 MINS COOK TIME: 25 MINS TOTAL TIME: 40 MINS

Ingredients

- Six medium sweet potatoes, cut into cubes and peels

- ¾ cup warm 2% milk, or more as required
- ½ cup pieces of softened butter
- 3/4 cup of maple syrup, or to taste

Directions

1. Prepare a generous pot of water with a touch of salt and bring it to a rolling boil. Simmer the sweet potatoes until tender, which should take about 20 to 30 minutes. Drain the contents and transfer them to a bowl.
2. Crush those potatoes using a potato masher. Gently incorporate 1/2 cup of warm milk at a time until you achieve the desired consistency. Combine the butter and maple syrup, stirring until they are thoroughly mixed and the butter has completely melted. Enjoy it while it's still nice and toasty.

CREAM OF MUSHROOM SOUP

PREP: 10 MINS COOK: 30 MINS TOTAL: 40 MINS

Ingredients

- four tsp of butter
- One spoonful of oil
- 2 chopped onions and 4 minced garlic cloves
- 1 1/2 pounds (750 g) fresh brown mushrooms sliced
- Four tsp finely chopped, split thyme
- Half a cup of dry red or white wine, or Marsala
- Six tablespoons of flour (all-purpose)
- Four cups low-sodium stock or broth for chicken
- One to two teaspoons of salt, or to taste
- Add one to two tablespoons of black pepper, ground to taste.
- Two crumbled beef bouillon cubes
- One cup heavy cream (or half-and-half; use evaporated milk as a substitute)
- chopped thyme and parsley for serving

Directions

1. Heat up the butter and oil in a spacious pot on medium-high heat until it's completely melted. Cook the onion over medium heat for 2 to 3 minutes until it becomes soft. Sauté the garlic until it becomes fragrant, which usually takes about a minute.
2. Include mushrooms and 2 teaspoons of thyme, then cook for 5 minutes. Add wine and let it cook for 3 minutes.

3. Coat the mushrooms with flour, ensuring they are well combined, and cook for a brief 2 minutes. Include stock, mix once more, and bring to a vigorous boil. Lower the heat to a gentle simmer and add a pinch of salt, a dash of pepper, and some crumbled bouillon cubes for flavor.
4. Make sure to cover the mixture and let it simmer for 10-15 minutes, giving it an occasional stir, until it thickens.
5. Lower the heat and gently incorporate cream or half and half. Let it gently simmer (avoid boiling). Feel free to customize the amount of salt and pepper to suit your personal preferences.
6. Incorporate the parsley and the rest of the thyme. Enjoy it while it's still nice and toasty.

Nutrition

Calories: 271kcal | Protein: 8g | Fiber: 1g | Sugar: 5g

COTTAGE CHEESE WITH FRUIT

PREP TIME 10 MINUTES TOTAL TIME 10 MINUTES SERVINGS 1

Ingredients
Sweeter Version:

- half a cup cottage cheese
- half a cup of fresh blueberries
- Half a cup of fresh strawberries plus five thinly sliced fresh mint leaves, diced and drizzled with honey

Savoury Version:

- half a cup cottage cheese
- half a cup of fresh blueberries
- 1/2 cup fresh + sliced strawberries
- Five tiny fresh basil leaves, finely chopped, with a drizzle of balsamic glaze
- Add black pepper to taste.

Directions

1. Place the cottage cheese gently into a bowl or cup.
2. Add a touch of freshness with some vibrant, seasonal fruit.
3. To add a touch of sweetness, you can garnish with some fresh mint leaves and a drizzle of honey.

4. To create a more flavorful variation, add some fresh basil, a generous drizzle of balsamic glaze, and a sprinkle of freshly cracked black pepper.
5. Combine all the ingredients and enjoy!

Notes

1. **PREPARE IN ADVANCE:** Although these recipes are most delicious when enjoyed immediately, you can certainly prepare them a day ahead. Ensure proper storage by placing the dish in an airtight container or covering the bowl before refrigerating.

CREAMY CARROT-GINGER SOUP

READY IN: 30MINS INGREDIENTS: 8

Ingredients

- three to four teaspoons vegetable oil
- Twelve chopped medium carrots (about five cups)
- 1/2 chopped onion (about a cup)
- two celery stalks, diced
- Two walnut-sized pieces of fresh ginger, peeled and mashed (or to taste)
- Two 14-ounce cans (or homemade) of chicken stock
- Three and a half cups heavy cream, salt, and pepper

Directions

1. Cook the carrots, onions, celery, and ginger in vegetable oil in a saucepan over medium heat until the vegetables have become tender, which should take around 10-12 minutes.
2. Include the chicken stock and bring it to a boil.
3. Include the cream and once more heat the soup until it reaches a boiling point. Then, lower the heat and allow it to simmer for 5 minutes.
4. Blend the soup until smooth, then strain it back into the saucepan.
5. Adjust the seasoning with salt and pepper according to your preference.

CREAMY MASHED POTATO

PREP: 10MINUTES COOK: 20MINUTES

Ingredients

- 1.5 kg / 3 lb potatoes, peeled and cut into 2.5cm/1" cubes
- 1 tablespoon of salt (for cooking)

Flavorings:

- 60 grams or 4 tablespoons unsalted butter, diced; 1/2 cup milk, preferably heated; and 1/2 teaspoon salt

Garnish:

- Extra butter that has melted
- chopped parsley or chives

Directions

1. Add 1 tbsp. of salt to a large pot. Ensure that the water level is 10cm / 4" above the potatoes.
2. Heat the mixture until it reaches a boiling point, then lower the heat to maintain a rapid simmer. Allow the potatoes to cook for approximately 15 minutes or until they reach a tender consistency. To check if they are ready, gently poke them with a fork - they should easily break apart.
3. Ensure thorough draining before returning to the pot. Allow to simmer for 1 minute, gently agitating the pot occasionally to aid in the reduction of liquid.
4. Enhance the taste by incorporating flavorings, then thoroughly mash the mixture until it reaches the desired consistency. You can add milk to loosen it up if a smoother texture is preferred.
5. Avoid using any mechanical device to mix or blend ingredients. It's important to exercise caution when using a stand mixer or handheld mixer to pulse the potatoes. Stop as soon as they reach a creamy consistency, as over-mixing can quickly turn them into a gluey mess.
6. Transfer the mixture to a serving bowl, creating elegant swirls across the top and delicately drizzling butter over it. Finish off with a sprinkle of fresh chives, and it's ready to be served!

Make Ahead Choose:

1. 30 minutes or less - Simply cover the bowl tightly with cling wrap and place it in a warm spot, such as near the stove. It will remain warm for the next 30 minutes. Delicately mix before serving.

2. Cook the mash for up to 2 hours by placing the bowl over a pot of boiling water. Remember to occasionally turn on the stove to keep the water hot, or keep it gently simmering with about 3 cm / 1" of water. Ensure that the bowl does not come into contact with the water.
3. For optimal results, set your slow cooker to the warm setting and let it work its magic for up to 4 hours. To ensure even cooking, gently press a sheet of baking paper or parchment paper onto the surface of the potatoes, and then tightly cover them with foil. Set your slow cooker to the WARM setting, keeping the temperature at 60C/140F or lower.

Notes

- When it comes to potatoes, it's important to choose the right ones. Floury potatoes are a great option, as they are versatile and can be used in a variety of dishes.
- Australia is known for its fantastic all-purpose potatoes, commonly referred to as Sebago. These cheap, dirt-brushed potatoes can be found everywhere and are a great choice for any dish.
- When using a handheld beater or kitchen stand mixer, it's important to be cautious. Beating potatoes too much can activate the starch, resulting in a gluey texture that is quite unpleasant. Whisking the ingredients will result in a velvety texture and a rich, indulgent creaminess. Perfection is elusive - the humble potato may transform into a sticky mess before achieving the desired smoothness.
- Creating a perfectly smooth mash requires a meticulous process that involves passing it through a fine sieve. This technique, commonly used in professional kitchens, requires specialized equipment and can be quite laborious.

Nutrition

Calories: 208cal | Carbohydrates: 29g | Protein: 6g | Fat: 8g | Fiber: 6g | Sugar: 1g Vitamin C: 26mg | Calcium: 86mg | Iron: 7mg

EASY CREAMY MUSHROOM AND SPINACH RISOTTO

PREP TIME 15 MINUTES COOK TIME 45 MINUTES TOTAL TIME 1 HOUR

Equipment

- One sizable saucepan
- One large Dutch oven or deep fryer

Ingredients

- One-liter water

- 2-3 tsp stock powder (for poultry, vegetables, etc.)
- One tablespoon of olive oil
- One large, finely sliced brown or yellow onion
- 400 g of sliced portobello mushrooms
- ½ teaspoon of freshly cut thyme stems
- two to three minced garlic cloves
- 1½ cups unwashed Arborio rice
- 125 ml of brandy or dry white wine
- ¼–½ cup finely grated parmesan cheese
- 1-2 tablespoons of evaporated milk or cream
- One to two teaspoons of lemon juice and zest
- two cups finely chopped spinach, about 1 tablespoon freshly chopped fresh parsley
- 1+ tsp freshly ground salt and pepper, to taste

Directions

1. Combine the water and stock powder in a large saucepan, stirring until well mixed. Bring the mixture to a boil. Lower the heat and maintain a gentle warmth on the stove.
2. In a large, deep-frying pan, heat the olive oil over medium heat. Add the onion and cook until it becomes transparent and begins to caramelize.
3. Incorporate the thyme, mushrooms, and garlic. Reduce the heat and continue stirring until the mushrooms have become tender and the garlic is cooked, which should take about 7 minutes.
4. Include the rice and toast it for 2-3 minutes, then pour in the wine and let it simmer until it evaporates. Make sure to stir continuously. Regularly stirring the rice while cooking helps to create a creamier texture by encouraging the grains to release starch.
5. After the wine has evaporated, you can start incorporating the warm stock gradually, using one ladle (or a half cup) at a time. Ensure that the rice is fully absorbing the liquid before proceeding to the next step, repeating the process until the rice is cooked through but still has a firm texture. It should take approximately 30 minutes. Adjust the flavour according to your preference.
6. The end product will have a luxuriously smooth sauce, even before incorporating the cheese and cream.
7. Incorporate the lemon juice, zest, cheese, cream, and spinach until they are gently wilted.
8. Take off the heat and add a pinch of salt and pepper to your liking. Add a touch of freshness and a sprinkle of savoury goodness.

Nutrition

Calories: 514kcal | Carbohydrates: 78g | Protein: 10g | Fat: 15g Fiber: 5g | Sugar: 7g | Vitamin C: 17mg | Calcium: 160mg | Iron: 4mg

HEALTHY MASHED SWEET POTATOES WITH GREEK YOGURT

PREP TIME 15MINUTES COOK TIME 25MINUTES TOTAL TIME 40MINUTES

Ingredients

- Three pounds of peeled sweet potatoes
- One tsp of extra virgin olive oil
- Half a chopped onion and two minced garlic cloves
- 1 tsp freshly chopped, finely chopped rosemary
- one-third cup Greek yogurt that is organic
- To taste, add salt and pepper.

Directions

1. Slice the sweet potatoes into small pieces, then place them in a steamer basket and steam for a little while, or until a fork can easily pierce them. Usually, this process takes twenty to twenty-five minutes.
2. In a medium, nonstick skillet, slowly warm the olive oil while the potatoes are cooking. Add the garlic and onions and cook, stirring occasionally, for about 8 minutes, or until fragrant and transparent.
3. In a medium bowl, combine the steamed sweet potatoes, Greek yogurt, onion and garlic mixture, and rosemary.
4. To improve the flavor, combine all the ingredients and season with a small pinch of salt and pepper. Taste the delicious flavors!

Notes

In the refrigerator, sweet potatoes that have been mashed can maintain their freshness for up to four days. In addition, they can be stored in the freezer for up to two months for subsequent use.

Nutrition

Serving: 0.75cup | Calories: 323kcal | Carbohydrates: 71g | Protein: 7g | Fat: 2g | Fiber: 10 g | Sugar: 16g

CREAMY BROCCOLI SOUP

15M PREP 35M COOK 4 SERVINGS

Ingredients

- Two teaspoons of olive oil
- One brown onion, cut finely
- two smashed garlic cloves
- one and a half broccoli heads, sliced stems and florets
- One Red Royale potato, diced and peeled
- Four mugs (1 liter) less-salted vegetable or poultry stock
- One cup, or 120 grams frozen peas
- 125ml, or half a cup, thickened cream

Parmesan wafers

- 120g/1 1/2 cups finely grated Parmesan cheese
- half a teaspoon of paprika

Directions

1. Heat up the oil in a spacious saucepan on a medium heat setting. Sauté the onion, stirring occasionally, for 5 minutes or until it becomes soft. Include the garlic and cook for about 30 seconds or until it becomes fragrant. Include the broccoli stems, potato, and stock, then bring the mixture to a boil. Continue cooking, stirring occasionally, for about 20 minutes or until the broccoli and potato reach a very tender consistency.
2. Include the broccoli florets and peas in the pan. Let it come to a gentle simmer. Prepare the dish for 3-5 minutes or until the vegetables reach a vibrant green colour and are cooked to a tender consistency. Take off the stove.
3. Utilize a stick blender to meticulously blend until achieving a smooth consistency. Mix in the cream until it is well incorporated. Flavor.
4. Meanwhile, for the parmesan wafers, preheat the oven to 200C. Prepare a baking tray by lining it with baking paper. Mix the parmesan and paprika in a spacious bowl. Distribute the ingredients evenly across the prepared tray. Add a touch of pepper for extra flavour. Cook for 2 minutes or until the parmesan becomes melted and has a golden colour. Allow it to cool. Break it apart.

5. Distribute the soup evenly into the serving bowls. Be sure to serve right away, accompanied by some delicious parmesan wafers.

AVOCADO EGG SALAD

PREP TIME10MINUTES TOTAL TIME10MINUTES SERVINGS4

Ingredients

- two sliced hard-cooked eggs
- 2 hard-boiled egg whites, diced; 2 pitted and skinned small avocados
- One tablespoon of Greek yogurt, plain
- One tablespoon of newly squeezed lemon juice
- two teaspoons of finely chopped green onion
- One-fourth teaspoon Dijon mustard
- To taste, add salt and freshly ground black pepper.

Directions

1. Combine the hard boiled eggs and egg whites, avocado, Greek yogurt, lemon juice, green onion, and mustard in a medium bowl.
2. Use a fork to mash until you achieve the texture you desire. Add a pinch of salt and pepper to enhance the flavour.

Nutrition

Calories: 211kcal, Carbohydrates: 9g, Protein: 7g, Fiber: 6g, Sugar: 1g, Vitamin C: 12mg

BUTTERNUT SQUASH RISOTTO

PREP TIME: 15MINUTES COOK TIME: 40MINUTES SERVES 4

Equipment

- Staub Dutch Oven
- Vegetable Broth
- Arborio Rice

Ingredients

- One tablespoon of pure olive oil
- 1/2 teaspoon sea salt and one medium yellow onion, diced, plus additional to taste

- freshly ground black pepper
- Two cups of ¼-inch diced butternut squash
- two cloves of coarsely chopped garlic
- 1 tsp finely chopped sage or rosemary
- One cup of raw Arborio rice and half a cup of dry white wine
- Four cups of heated vegetable stock
- Garnish with chopped parsley or tiny sage leaves, if desired.
- For serving, you can add ½ cup of grated Pecorino or Parmesan cheese.

Instructions

1. Heat the oil in a large skillet over medium heat. Sauté the onion with a pinch of salt and a generous amount of freshly ground pepper, cooking it for 2 to 3 minutes. Include the butternut squash and cook for 6 to 8 minutes.
2. Incorporate the garlic, rosemary, and rice. Mix and allow to cook for approximately 1 minute before adding the wine. Continuously stir and cook the mixture for 1 to 3 minutes or until the wine reduces.
3. Incorporate the broth gradually, adding ¾ cup at a time, while stirring consistently to ensure each portion is fully absorbed before introducing the next. Ensure the butternut squash is cooked until tender and the risotto reaches a soft and creamy consistency. Adjust the seasoning according to your preference.
4. Add a touch of elegance to your dish by garnishing it with fresh parsley or sage leaves. For an extra indulgent experience, you can also serve it with a sprinkle of grated cheese. Enjoy!

BANANA OATMEAL

ACTIVE TIME: 20 MINS TOTAL TIME: 20 MINS

Ingredients

- Four big, ripe bananas, divided; three cups of skim milk
- Two cups of traditional rolled oats
- Three teaspoons of pure maple syrup
- ¾ teaspoon ground cinnamon, with additional for sprinkling; 1 teaspoon vanilla extract
- 1/4 tsp ground ginger
- One-half teaspoon of salt

Directions

1. Peel and slice one banana, set it aside for serving. With a fork, gently mash the remaining 3 bananas in a large saucepan. Include milk and heat the mixture until it simmers, making sure to frequently scrape the bottom of the pan with a wooden spoon. Mix in oats, maple syrup, vanilla, cinnamon, ginger, and salt. Lower the heat to a gentle simmer. Continue cooking, making sure to scrape the bottom of the pan frequently with the spoon until the mixture reaches a thick and creamy consistency, which should take approximately 5 minutes. Evenly distribute the oatmeal into 4 bowls and carefully place the banana slices on top. Feel free to add a touch of cinnamon if you'd like, and enjoy right away.

Tips

For people who have celiac disease or gluten sensitivity, it is important to opt for oats that are specifically labelled as "gluten-free." This is because oats are frequently exposed to wheat and barley, leading to potential cross-contamination.

TROPICAL FRUIT BAKED OATMEAL

PREP TIME: 10MINUTES COOK TIME: 45MINUTES SERVINGS: 4 CALORIES: 326KCAL

Equipment

- baking dish, casserole dish, pie plate
- mixing bowl

Ingredients

- Two overripe bananas
- One-fourth cup of plain applesauce
- Two tablespoons of cane sugar
- One teaspoon almond extract
- A half-tsp of baking powder
- 1/4 teaspoon grated ginger
- 1/4 teaspoon kosher salt
- One cup of unsweetened almond milk, cashew milk, or skim
- 1.5 cups of traditional oatmeal

Topping

- Two cups of pineapple chunks; drain the liquid if using canned pineapple.

- Two cups of chunky mangos—make sure to thaw if using frozen ones—
- One teaspoon corn starch
- 3/4 cup of coconut flakes with sugar

Instructions

1. Set the oven temperature to 375F.
2. Place the mango and pineapple chunks into a small saucepan.
3. Heat the mixture over medium-high heat for 5 minutes.
4. Incorporate the cornstarch into the mixture, ensuring it blends well with the fruit and its juices.
5. Keep cooking for an additional 5 minutes or until the mango has completely softened and the mixture has reached a thick consistency. The pineapple will remain intact.
6. Prepare a small baking dish or casserole by applying a light coating of cooking spray. I used a standard-sized casserole dish for this recipe.
7. Place the bananas in the bottom of a mixing bowl and use a fork to mash them.
8. Combine the applesauce, sugar, baking powder, salt, extract, and ground ginger by stirring them together.
9. Please include the milk. Mix together.
10. Include the oats. Incorporate gently.
11. Ensure that the mixture is distributed evenly throughout the baking dish.
12. Place the fruit mixture on top and generously sprinkle with the coconut.
13. Set the oven temperature to 375 and bake for 35 minutes.

CREAMY CHICKEN AND RICE

PREP 25MINUTES COOK 10MINUTES TOTAL 35MINUTES

Ingredients

- One pound of tiny, bite-sized chicken breast chunks
- One teaspoon of paprika sweet
- one tsp powdered garlic
- One tsp powdered onion
- Two teaspoons of unsalted butter
- one big sliced onion
- three minced garlic cloves
- One spoonful of seasoning from Italy
- One cup long-grain rice, such jasmine rice
- 2 cups low-sodium chicken broth

- To taste, add salt and pepper.
- One cup of heavy cream
- One cup of freshly grated Parmesan cheese
- arugula fresh (for garnish)

Instructions

1. Improve the flavour of the chicken by adding a touch of sweet paprika, garlic powder, and onion powder. Put it aside.
2. Heat the butter in a large skillet over medium heat. Sauté the onion until it becomes soft and translucent, which usually takes about 3 minutes. Include the garlic and continue cooking for an additional 30 seconds until it becomes fragrant.
3. Place the chicken into the skillet and cook it for about 5 minutes until it is no longer pink.
4. Include a generous amount of Italian seasoning, along with rice and chicken broth, and season the mixture with a pinch of salt and pepper. Heat the mixture until it starts boiling, then lower the temperature and cover the skillet with a lid. Allow the rice to cook undisturbed for 15 minutes.
5. Incorporate the rich cream and tangy Parmesan cheese into the mixture, allowing the rice to soak up the flavours for a few additional minutes. Ensure the flavours are perfectly balanced by adjusting the seasoning with salt and pepper, if necessary.
6. Finish off with a sprinkle of fresh parsley and serve right away.

Notes

1. It's important to give the rice a good rinse before cooking. To achieve a more delicate texture, it is advisable to rinse the uncooked rice in a strainer using cool running water. This process will effectively eliminate any remaining starch or debris.
2. Please refrain from disturbing the lid. No need to constantly stir the rice or check its progress. Ensuring a tight seal on the skillet lid is essential during the 15-minute steaming process for the rice.
3. Finish with seasoning at the end. Ensure that no additional salt is added until the dish is fully prepared and ready to be served. The chicken stock and parmesan cheese add a generous amount of flavour to the rice.
4. Leftover creamy chicken and rice can be stored in an airtight container in the refrigerator for up to 5 days.

CAULIFLOWER PURÉE WITH THYME

SERVINGS: 4 PREP TIME: 5 MINUTES COOK TIME: 20 MINUTES

TOTAL TIME: 25 MINUTES

Ingredients

- One 2-pound head of cauliflower, chopped into ½-inch pieces (florets not necessary to be kept whole).
- One cup of chicken broth
- One tsp salt and more to taste
- Three tablespoons of chunky unsalted butter
- One teaspoon of freshly chopped thyme
- freshly ground peppercorns, according to taste

Instructions

1. Bring the chicken broth and salt to a boil in a large pot. Include the cauliflower and bring it back to a boil. Simply cover the pot, lower the heat, and let the cauliflower steam for about 20 minutes until it becomes wonderfully tender. Transfer the cauliflower to a food processor using a slotted spoon. Incorporate 3 tablespoons of chicken broth from the pot, along with the butter. Blend until silky. Ensure the flavours are perfectly balanced by adding a pinch of salt and a sprinkle of freshly ground pepper. Incorporate thyme into the mixture, processing until it is just blended.

CHAPTER 4: PUREED FOOD RECIPES

CAULIFLOWER PURÉE WITH THYME

PREP TIME: 5 MINUTES COOK TIME: 20 MINUTES TOTAL TIME: 25 MINUTES
SERVINGS: 4

Ingredients

- One 2-pound head of cauliflower, chopped into ½-inch pieces (florets not necessary to be kept whole).
- One cup of chicken broth
- One tsp salt and more to taste
- Three tablespoons of chunky unsalted butter
- One teaspoon of freshly chopped thyme
- freshly ground peppercorns, according to taste

Instructions

1. Bring the chicken broth and salt to a boil in a large pot. Include the cauliflower and bring it back to a boil. Simply cover and simmer on low heat for 20 minutes, until the cauliflower becomes incredibly tender. Transfer the cauliflower to a food processor using a slotted spoon. Incorporate 3 tablespoons of chicken broth from the pot, along with the butter. Blend until silky. Ensure the flavours are perfectly balanced by adding a pinch of salt and a sprinkle of freshly ground pepper. Incorporate thyme into the mixture, being careful not to over-mix.

MASHED SWEET POTATOES

Ingredients

- Three pounds of sweet potatoes, medium-sized (3 or 4)
- Half a cup unsalted butter
- Six tablespoons of pure maple syrup
- Half a cup of milk
- A quarter of a teaspoon each of salt and freshly ground black pepper
- For serving, fresh thyme leaves (optional)

Instructions

1. Ensure that the oven is preheated to 350°F and position an oven rack in the middle. Prepare a baking sheet with foil to make clean-up a breeze.

2. Using a fork, make small punctures in each sweet potato about 3 to 4 times. Put them on the baking sheet and bake until they're tender, which should take about 60 to 75 minutes. Remember to flip the potatoes over halfway through baking.
3. Meanwhile, heat up the butter in a medium saucepan over medium heat. Incorporate the maple syrup, milk, salt, and pepper. Switch off the stove and set it aside.
4. Once the sweet potatoes are cooked and have cooled down, simply cut them in half. With a firm grip and a protective mitt, carefully transfer the heated flesh into the pan along with the butter mixture. Gently heat the potatoes and use a masher or fork to create a smooth consistency. Ensure the flavors are perfectly balanced by tasting and making any necessary adjustments to the seasoning. Place the mixture into a bowl and add a touch of fresh thyme, if desired. Ensure the dish is served piping hot.
5. **Just a heads up:** You can prepare these sweet potatoes in advance. Prior to serving, incorporate a small amount of milk and warm it up on the stovetop or in the microwave.

BROCCOLI PURÉE

SERVINGS: 6 TO 8

Ingredients

- Divided 4 tablespoons unsalted butter; add extra to serve if preferred.
- One small onion yields ½ cup of chopped yellow onion.
- Half a cup of water
- One tsp salt and more to taste
- Twenty milligrams of newly ground black pepper
- Two pounds of floretized broccoli crowns with the rough stalks thinly chopped
- ¼ cup sour cream; 1 tablespoon fresh thyme leaves
- For serving, use one tablespoon of finely chopped chives.

Instructions

1. In a pot large enough to hold all of the broccoli, melt half of the butter over medium heat. Sauté the onions until they become soft, stirring often, for about 3 to 4 minutes. Combine the water, salt, and pepper by stirring with a wooden spoon. Include the broccoli and bring the liquid to a boil. Ensure the pot is tightly covered and lower the heat to a simmer. Ensure the broccoli is cooked until it reaches a tender consistency, which typically takes around 15 minutes.
2. Move everything from the pot, including the liquid, into a food processor that has the steel blade attached. Incorporate the remaining butter and thyme into the mixture, processing until it reaches a slightly coarse texture. Incorporate the sour cream and

process once more until achieving a smooth consistency. Make sure to taste the dish and make any necessary adjustments to the salt level. In my experience, adding an extra ¾ teaspoon of salt usually does the trick. Place the dish in a serving bowl, and add a dollop of butter, if desired, along with some chives for garnish. (Please be aware that if your food processor is on the smaller side, you might have to work in multiple batches.)

- **Reminder:** It's important to thinly slice the tough stems so that they can cook properly.
- **Preparation Tips:** You can prepare the purée in advance and store it in the refrigerator for up to 3 days. Warm up using either the microwave or stovetop.

CHICKEN, RICE, AND CARROT PUREE

YIELD: 8-10 SERVINGS PREP TIME: 10 MINUTES TOTAL TIME: 10 MINUTES

Ingredients

- Half a cup of cooked chicken, sliced finely
- One-third cup chicken broth
- 1/3 cup of rice
- Two carrots, peeled and cooked and chopped into bits
- 1/4 cup applesauce
- One tspn of sage or rosemary

Instructions

1. Blend the chicken and chicken broth in a blender until it becomes a smooth mixture.
2. Include the rice, carrots, applesauce, and choose between rosemary or sage. Mix until you achieve the texture you want. Feel free to add additional liquid if necessary.
3. Ensure optimal freshness by consuming within three days or alternatively, freeze in convenient two-ounce portions and enjoy within a span of two months.

HOMEMADE SWEET POTATO PUREE

PREP TIME: 10MINUTES COOK TIME: 45MINUTES TOTAL TIME: 55MINUTES
SERVINGS: 4 CUPS

Ingredients

- 6 medium sweet potatoes
- Cook Mode Prevents your screen from going dark while preparing the recipe.

Instructions

1. Thoroughly clean the sweet potatoes and ensure they are completely dry. Poke the sweet potatoes with a fork multiple times.
2. For oven-roasted sweet potatoes, simply arrange your sweet potatoes on a sheet pan covered with foil. Cook at 400 degrees F until the potatoes are incredibly tender and the flesh easily yields to a fork. It should take around 45-50 minutes to cook the sweet potatoes until they are medium in texture. Cooking times for sweet potatoes vary depending on their size. Smaller sweet potatoes typically take around 35-40 minutes to cook, while larger ones require 60-65 minutes.
3. To cook sweet potatoes in an Instant Pot, simply set them on a trivet within the inner pot of an electric pressure cooker. This will allow the potatoes to cook as quickly as possible. For an Instant Pot model with a capacity of 6 quarts, add one cup of cold water, while for an Instant Pot model with a capacity of 8 quarts, add one and a half cups of cold water.
4. Set the cooking time to 18 minutes for small potatoes, 22 minutes for standard ones, and 27 minutes for large ones. After the cooking time is up, allow the pressure to naturally release for 10 minutes.
5. Once the sweet potatoes are cooked, it's best to let them cool down a bit before handling.
6. Peel off the skins from the sweet potatoes and transfer the flesh into a food processor equipped with an s-blade or a high-powered blender. Blend the sweet potato puree until it becomes velvety and luscious.

Equipment Needed

- Food Processor

Notes

- Approximately half a cup of sweet potato puree can be obtained from each medium-sized sweet potato. The amount of sweet potato puree that may be obtained from larger sweet potatoes is closer to one cup.
- When you are pureeing the sweet potatoes for baby food, you might want to add a little bit of purified water, formula, breast milk, or apple juice that is 100 percent to make them a little bit more liquid.
- The sweet potato puree should be allowed to cool before being stored in an airtight container for a period of up to five days once it has been stored. Another option is to place the pureed mixture in a container that is safe for freezing and store it in the freezer for up to three months. Allow it defrost in the refrigerator for a whole night, and then use as you like.

Nutrition

Calories: 292kcal | Carbohydrates: 68g | Protein: 5g | Fat: 0.2g | Saturated Fat: 0.1g | Sugar: 14g | Iron: 2mg

APPLE PUREE / SAUCE

PREP TIME: 15MINUTES COOK TIME: 15MINUTES TOTAL TIME: 30MINUTES

Ingredients

- Peel, core, and chop six medium apples into bits.
- 60 milliliters (¼ cup) of water ¼ teaspoon of ground cinnamon

Instructions

1. Put every ingredient into a saucepan with a thick bottom.
2. Cook, covered, on low heat for 15 to 20 minutes, or until tender.
3. Use a food processor, hand blender, or blender to puree.

Recipe Notes

1. I absolutely adore the Kanji or Pink Lady apple varieties, so they are my go-to choices. Some other excellent choices are McIntosh, Cortland, Fuji, Golden Delicious, Jazz, Royal Gala, and Jonathan. Adding cinnamon is up to you. Consider omitting or substituting spices like ginger, nutmeg, star anise, or vanilla.
2. If you like a denser texture, you can opt for mashing instead of pureeing by using a fork or potato masher.

Nutritional Facts

Calories: 95kcal | Carbohydrates: 25g | Protein: 0g | Fat: 0g | Fiber: 4g | Sugar: 18g | Vitamin C: 8.3mg | Calcium: 13mg | Iron: 0.2mg

CLASSIC PUREED TUNA SALAD

PREP TIME 5 MINUTES TOTAL TIME 5 MINUTES

Ingredients

- One 6-ounce can of tuna sealed in water
- two tsp of relish

- One or two teaspoons reduced-fat mayonnaise
- Two teaspoons of Icelandic or plain Greek yogurt
- If preferred, add salt and pepper to taste.

Instructions

1. Combine the tuna chunks and relish in a compact food processor.
2. Blend the tuna until the meat is finely shredded.
3. Place the shredded tuna/relish mixture into a mixing bowl.
4. Mix together the mayonnaise and yoghurt with the tuna mixture.
5. Blend together all the ingredients.
6. Feel free to add some salt and pepper for extra flavor, if you'd like.
7. Portion the dish into ¼ cup (2 oz) servings.

Nutrition

Serving: 1/4 cup Calories: 78kcal Carbohydrates: 1.7g Protein: 10.5g Fat: 2.9g Fiber: 0g Sugar: 1.1g

PUREED CARROT SOUP

TOTAL TIME ABOUT 1 HOUR YIELD: SERVES 6

Ingredients

- One teaspoon of unsalted butter
- One teaspoon of extra virgin olive oil
- One large onion, diced; two pounds of peeled and thinly sliced sweet carrots
- A teaspoon of sugar and salt to taste
- Two quarts of water, vegetable stock, or chicken stock
- Six tablespoons of rice
- freshly ground pepper according to taste
- For garnish, add two tablespoons of finely chopped fresh herbs, like parsley, chives, mint, or chervil.
- One cup of toasted croutons as a garnish

Preparation

1. Warm up the butter and olive oil in a spacious soup pot on a gentle flame, then add the onion. Continue cooking, stirring occasionally, until the ingredients are tender, which should take around 5 minutes. Include the carrots and ½ teaspoon of salt, partially cover, and cook for an additional 10 minutes, stirring frequently, until the vegetables

become tender and release a delightful aroma. Incorporate the rice, water or stock, salt (approximately 1½ teaspoons), and sugar. Heat the mixture until it reaches a boiling point, then lower the temperature and let it simmer for about 30 minutes. This will allow the carrots to become soft and the soup to develop a delightful aroma.
2. Puree the soup using a hand blender, a blender (remember to cover the top and hold it down to prevent any hot splashes), or a food mill with the fine blade. The rice should be completely transformed, adding thickness to the soup. Get back to the pot. Mix and sample. Season with salt, sprinkle a liberal amount of freshly ground pepper, and warm until heated. If you want to enhance the sweetness of the carrots, consider adding a little extra sugar.
3. Present each bowl with a delightful touch of croutons and a delicate sprinkle of herbs.

Tip

1. Alternative: Use a medium Yukon gold potato or half a russet potato (around 5 ounces), peeled and diced, instead of the rice. Preparation in advance: You have the option to prepare the soup in advance and simply reheat it when needed. This allows for flexibility in your meal planning and ensures that the soup is still delicious and ready to serve.

TURKEY GRAVY AND GARLIC POTATO PURÉE

SERVINGS 16 PREP TIME 15 MINUTES COOK TIME 30 MINUTESCALORIES 248

Ingredients

- Half a cup (2 oz/55 g) of butter or turkey fat
- 2/3 cup flour (2 oz/55 g)
- One-quart heated turkey drippings and stock
- Add black pepper as needed.
- Honorable Salt functions. Hickory smoked salt when necessary

Garlic Potato Purée Recipe

- 2 pounds of peeled russet potatoes
- four peeled garlic cloves
- One cup of butter
- One cup of heavy cream
- Noble Salt is effective. To taste, Hickory Smoked Salt

Directions

1. Heat up your turkey fat and/or butter in a Lodge 12" Cast Iron Skillet over medium heat. Whisk in the flour until it's fully incorporated. Keep whisking as the roux cooks, for approximately one minute, until it turns a slightly brown color and releases a delightful aroma.
2. Gently pour the turkey drippings and turkey stock into the skillet, whisking continuously, until fully combined. Let the gravy gently simmer. Reduce the temperature. Prepare the dish to your preferred texture.
3. Flavour and season with a touch of black pepper and salt, as required.

Garlic Potato Purée Recipe

1. Cut the potatoes into 2" pieces. Put it in a pot of cool water. Include the cloves of garlic. Heat until it reaches a boiling point. Bring the heat down to a gentle simmer. Ensure the potatoes are cooked until they are tender when pierced with a skewer. Remove the excess water.
2. In another pot, gently heat the butter and cream until they reach a simmer. Pour the liquid into the potatoes. Blend until smooth using an immersion blender or hand mixer. Enhance the flavor with the exquisite touch of Noble Salt's Hickory Smoked Salt.

PERFECT BANANA & AVOCADO PURÉE

PREP: 5 MINS SERVES 1 (BABY), NO-COOK

Ingredients

- ½ ripe tiny avocado
- One tiny, ripe banana
- One tablespoon yogurt (optional)

Method

1. Divide the avocado in half, take out the pit, and scoop out the middle. Place it in the baby's bowl.
2. Combine the banana and avocado and mash them together.
3. If your little one has developed a taste for smoother textures, you might consider adding a bit more texture to their meals.
4. If you're looking to introduce your little one to some protein, why not try stirring it into some yogurt? Make sure to serve immediately.

CHICKEN & MIXED VEG PURÉE

PREP: 5 MINS COOK: 10 MINS MAKES ABOUT 500G

Ingredients

- One tiny sweet potato (about 150g), peeled and sliced
- one chicken breast, chopped into pieces
- One small (about 150g) courgette, chopped into pieces
- Four florets of broccoli
- Two tablespoons of plain yogurt
- infant milk

Method

1. Place the sweet potato in a saucepan of medium size and cover it with water. Heat the mixture until it reaches a boiling point and let it simmer for 3 minutes. After that, include the chicken, courgette, and broccoli and continue simmering for approximately 7 minutes until the chicken is fully cooked and the vegetables are tender.
2. After draining, you can transfer the mixture to a food processor along with the yogurt. Blend until creamy, gradually adding milk to achieve desired consistency. After preparing a delicious meal, it's a good idea to portion out one serving and store the remaining portions in small containers to freeze for later.

CREAMY MUSHROOM SOUP

PREP TIME15MINUTES COOK TIME1HOUR 10MINUTES TOTAL TIME1HOUR 25MINUTES

Ingredients

- Turmeric, three tablespoons of extra virgin
- Three tsp unsalted butter
- Sliced cremini mushrooms, 2.5 pounds; see notes below.
- One big white onion, chopped; three ribs chopped celery, five minced garlic cloves
- 1/4 cup of flour for all purposes
- one-third cup of dry white wine
- Four cups low-sodium chicken stock + additional, if necessary, to thin
- One tablespoon of newly plucked thyme
- One big bay leaf and one cup of heavy cream
- To taste, add salt and pepper.

Instructions

1. Prepare a large, heavy pot by heating it slightly above medium heat with a combination of butter and olive oil. Incorporate the mushrooms, generously season with salt, and cook until they release their moisture and develop a golden hue (20-25 minutes). Be prepared to invest a significant amount of time due to the abundance of mushrooms.
2. After that, incorporate the celery and onion into the mixture and keep cooking for approximately 10 additional minutes or until the vegetables have become tender. Include the garlic and continue cooking for an additional 2 minutes.
3. Ensure the flour is thoroughly cooked until there are no white specks remaining (1-2 minutes).
4. Include the white wine and bring it to a boil. Using a wooden spoon, gently scrape the bottom of the pot to release all of the flavorful remnants. Once the water has been boiling for a minute, go ahead and add in the chicken stock, thyme, and bay leaf. Bring the mixture to a boil. After reaching a boiling point, reduce the heat and let it simmer for 45 minutes.
5. Once the simmering is complete, it's time to remove the bay leaf and blend the soup into a smooth puree. Pour the soup into a blender or utilize an immersion blender. For a more rustic soup, consider leaving some of the soup unblended.
6. Incorporate the cream thoroughly for a well-blended mixture. Conduct a taste test and make any necessary adjustments to the levels of salt and pepper. If the soup is too thick, you can easily adjust the consistency by adding more stock or water.
7. Enhance the dish with some crispy croutons, a touch of extra virgin olive oil or creme fraiche, and a sprinkle of fresh thyme for added flavor. Have a great time!

Notes

1. Cremini mushrooms are easily found and are a great choice for this soup. However, if you prefer, you can experiment with a variety of unique mushrooms. This soup becomes even more delightful with the addition of porcini mushrooms.
2. Adding greens such as escarole, spinach, or kale can bring a vibrant touch to the soup.
3. When preparing a vegetarian dish, opting for vegetable or mushroom stock is a great choice.
4. Leftovers can be safely stored in the refrigerator for up to three days and easily reheated either on the stovetop or in the microwave.

Nutrition

Calories: 292kcal | Carbohydrates: 16.3g | Protein: 8.8g |Sugar: 5.4g | Calcium: 33mg

YOGURT AND FRUIT PURÉE BREAKFAST

Ingredients

- 400 grams of natural, full-fat Greek-style yogurt
- 320 g of any mix of fruits, such as bananas, blueberries, strawberries, raspberries, or dessert apples either frozen or fresh
- two to four tablespoons of water
- 75 grams of rolled oats
- Optional: ¼ teaspoon ground cinnamon
- 1 tablespoon of dried coconut or linseed mixture
- Chopped hazelnuts (50 g)
- To garnish, use fresh blueberries

Instructions

1. Get your fruit ready if you're using fresh fruit. For example, peel, core, and roughly chop apples, peel and slice bananas, and hull berries.
2. Put the fruit in a saucepan along with the water. Heat the mixture gently for a few minutes until it reaches a simmering point, creating a smooth purée. Handle with care.
3. Combine the oats, cinnamon (if desired), coconut or linseed mix, and nuts. For added flavour and texture, you can lightly toast these ingredients in a non-stick frying pan over medium heat. Divide 4 dessert spoons of yogurt evenly among 4 wine or sundae dishes. Add a generous amount of the fruit purée followed by a generous portion of the crunchy oat mixture. Continue layering and top it off with a generous amount of fresh berries.

CARROT-GINGER PUREE

HANDS-ON: 25 MINS TOTAL: 55 MINS YIELD: MAKES 6 TO 8 SERVINGS

Ingredients

- Two pounds of roughly chopped carrots (approximately four cups)
- Two cups sugar, two cups milk
- 1/2 tsp. ground ginger or 2 tablespoons freshly grated ginger
- One tablespoonful of salt
- ⅛ teaspoon of cinnamon powder
- One spoonful of butter
- One tsp lightly packed orange peel

Directions

- Heat the carrots and milk in a saucepan until they come to a boil. Lower the heat and gently mix in the sugar and the following three ingredients. Carefully cook, stirring frequently, for 25 minutes or until the carrots have reached a tender consistency.
- Move the mixture to a blender, keeping aside 1/2 cup of the cooking liquid. Incorporate butter and orange zest into the carrot mixture, blending until it reaches a smooth consistency. Remember to pause and scrape down the sides as necessary. Gradually add reserved cooking liquid, if needed, 1 tablespoon at a time, and blend until you achieve the desired texture. Ensure prompt service or enjoy it cold. Make sure to store it in a sealed container in the refrigerator for a maximum of three days.
- Reminder: Simmering may cause curdling in organic milk. Rest assured, the texture will become velvety once it's blended.

CREAMY BUTTERNUT SQUASH SOUP RECIPE

PREP TIME: 10MINUTES COOK TIME: 20MINUTES 0MINUTES TOTAL TIME: 30MINUTES SERVINGS: 6

Ingredients

- Three pounds of diced butternut squash
- Three teaspoons of olive oil
- Two cups of chicken or vegetable stock, or more if necessary
- One large carrot, sliced and peeled
- One green apple, cut and peeled
- One chopped and seeded red bell pepper
- One sliced white or yellow onion
- One tsp salt, or to taste; one-third teaspoon pepper, or to taste
- One-half teaspoon of optional smoked paprika
- Two 15-oz cans of coconut milk without sugar
- garnishes that are optional: black pepper, parmesan cheese, smoked paprika, pepitas or roasted pumpkin seeds, dried cranberries, sunflower seeds, parsley or thyme

Instructions

1. Heat olive oil in a large stockpot and add a medley of butternut squash, carrot, apple, bell pepper, garlic, onion, and celery. Cook for 3-4 minutes until the garlic becomes fragrant and the onions turn translucent.

2. Include some stock, salt and pepper, and smoked paprika (if desired) and bring the mixture to a boil. Simmer the mixture for 5-10 minutes on medium heat until the vegetables and squash become wonderfully tender.
3. Incorporate the coconut milk. Blend the mixture until it becomes smooth and creamy, either using an immersion blender or by transferring it in batches to a high-powered blender.
4. Flavor, adjust with a sprinkle of salt and pepper if desired. You may want to consider adding a bit more stock or water to thin the mixture, if necessary. Feel free to add your own personal touch to the presentation and serve.

Nutrition

Calories: 204 kcal, Protein: 3 g, Sugar: 11 g

GREEK YOGHURT BERRY SMOOTHIE

PREP TIME: 5MINUTES MINS SERVING SIZE: 1

Ingredients:

- ¾ cup milk (dairy, rice, oat, almond, etc.)
- One ripe banana
- ½ cup of frozen berry mixture
- ½ cup Greek yogurt, plain
- One tablespoon of chia seeds
- One teaspoon honey

Method:

Add all ingredients into a blender and process until smooth.

Notes:

- For A Thinner Smoothie: Add A Bit More Liquid Until You Reach Your Desired Consistency.
- Dairy-Free or Vegan? Substitute For Coconut Yoghurt – This Will Lower The Protein Content And Increase The Fat Content.

CHAPTER 5: LIQUID FOOD RECIPES

CREAMY POTATO SOUP

PREP TIME 20 MINUTES COOK TIME 30 MINUTES TOTAL TIME 50 MINUTES

SERVINGS 4

Equipment

- Large Pot
- Potato Masher

Ingredients

- six bacon pieces, diced
- Diced ½ white onion finely
- four minced garlic cloves
- ¼ cup flour for all purposes
- Two cups of chicken stock or broth
- two cups of whole milk
- Two pounds of Yukon gold or red potatoes
- One cup of sharp cheddar cheese, shredded
- half a cup of sour cream
- ¼ cup finely chopped chives
- Taste-tested Kosher salt
- To taste, add black pepper.

Instructions

1. Begin by peeling the potatoes and then proceed to cut them into ½-inch cubes.
2. In a soup pot or Dutch oven, cook the bacon until it becomes wonderfully crispy over medium heat. Remove the bacon from the pot and place it on a plate lined with paper towels, allowing the excess fat to remain in the pot.
3. Place the onions into the bacon fat and gently cook over a medium heat until they start to soften, taking care not to let them brown. This should take around 4 to 5 minutes. Add the garlic and continue cooking for an additional minute until it becomes fragrant.
4. Add the flour and whisk until well combined (the mixture will become thick). Prepare the dish for 1 minute, ensuring to stir consistently.
5. Add the chicken stock and milk gradually, whisking until smooth after each addition. Include the potatoes and let them simmer on medium heat.

6. Lower the heat to medium-low and simmer the potatoes gently, stirring occasionally until they become soft, which should take around 15 to 20 minutes. Make sure the mixture doesn't reach boiling point to prevent the milk from burning.
7. Once the potatoes are tender, gently mash some of them with a potato masher to achieve a creamy texture.
8. Take it off the heat and mix in the shredded cheese, sour cream, chives, and half of the crispy bacon. Ensure to add the perfect balance of salt and pepper to enhance the flavor. Finish off with the rest of the bacon.

Notes

1. For optimal results, it is recommended to use uncooked bacon in this recipe. When utilizing pre-cooked bacon, sauté the onions in butter seasoned with a pinch of salt.
2. Yukon gold potatoes would be a fantastic addition to this recipe. While russet potatoes can be used, it's important to note that they have a slightly grainy texture that may alter the soup's consistency.
3. For a velvety texture, consider mashing or gently blending some of the potatoes with an immersion blender.
4. You can thicken the soup by mashing additional potatoes or incorporating potato flakes.
5. Ensure that the potato soup is properly stored in a covered container in the refrigerator for a maximum of 3-4 days. Warm up using either the stovetop or the microwave.

Nutrition

Calories: 484.87 | Protein: 20.02g | Fiber: 4.36g | Sugar: 12.64g | Iron: 2.56mg

STRAWBERRY BANANA SMOOTHIE

PREP TIME: 5 MINUTES TOTAL TIME: 5 MINUTES YIELD: ABOUT 2 SERVINGS

Ingredients

- Two cups of strawberries, frozen
- One banana, yet unpeeled
- One cup of milk (almond milk was used)
- one cup of ice

Instructions

1. Mix. Combine all the ingredients in a blender and blend until you achieve a smooth consistency. If the consistency appears too thick, you can incorporate some additional

milk or water. If the consistency appears to be too thin, you can incorporate additional strawberries or banana to enhance the texture.
2. Present. Make sure to serve right away and savour every bite!

TOMATO BASIL SOUP

PREP TIME: 15MINUTES COOK TIME: 1HOUR 30MINUTES SERVES 6 TO 8

Ingredients

- One-half cup extra-virgin olive oil and two and a half pounds of roma tomatoes, divided
- Chop one medium yellow onion and one-third cup of sliced carrots.
- 4 chopped garlic cloves and 3 cups of vegetable broth
- One-third cup balsamic vinegar
- One tsp of fresh thyme
- 1 cup loosely packed basil leaves; more for decoration
- freshly ground black pepper and sea salt

Instructions

1. Make sure to preheat the oven to 350°F and prepare a large baking sheet by lining it with parchment paper. Arrange the tomatoes with the cut side facing up on the baking sheet. Gently pour 2 tablespoons of olive oil over them and season with a pinch of salt and pepper. Cook for approximately 1 hour, or until the edges begin to slightly shrivel and the insides remain moist.
2. Warm up the remaining 2 tablespoons of olive oil in a large pot over medium heat. Sauté the onions, carrots, garlic, and a pinch of salt until they become tender, which should take around 8 minutes. Add the tomatoes, vegetable broth, vinegar, and thyme leaves to the mixture and let it simmer for 20 minutes.
3. Allow the soup to cool for a moment, then transfer it to a blender, if needed, blending in small portions at a time. Puree until velvety. Incorporate the basil into the mixture by pulsing until it is well combined.
4. Enhance the soup's presentation by adding fresh basil leaves and pair it with a delightful slice of crusty bread.

CARROT GINGER SOUP

PREP: 30MINUTES COOK: 30MINUTES TOTAL: 1HOUR SERVINGS: 4

Ingredients

- Two tablespoons of olive or avocado oil
- One medium onion, chopped; three minced garlic cloves; and three tablespoons of finely chopped or minced ginger
- Two pounds of chopped and peeled carrots
- Four cups of broth made with vegetables
- One bay leaf
- One tsp of cinnamon
- One tsp salt
- Topping options include toasted pine nuts, cilantro, coconut cream, and crispy shallots.

Instructions

1. Warm up the oil on the stove in a big pot. Sauté the onions until they become translucent, typically within 1 to 2 minutes.
2. Incorporate the ginger and garlic into the pot, stirring for an additional minute.
3. Add the diced carrots to the pot and gently mix them together. Prepare the dish for a duration of 10 minutes, ensuring to stir frequently.
4. Incorporate the broth, bay leaf, cinnamon, and salt into the pot. Heat the mixture until it reaches a boiling point, then reduce the heat and cover to maintain a gentle simmer. Allow the dish to cook for 20-30 minutes or until the carrots have reached a soft and tender texture when tested with a fork.
5. Please remember to turn off the heat and remove the bay leaf. Puree the soup using either an immersion blender or by transferring it to a high-powered blender. Puree the soup until it's smooth and velvety.
6. Separate the soup into individual bowls. For an added touch, you can drizzle a tablespoon of coconut cream on the surface and embellish it with crunchy shallots, toasted pine nuts, and fresh cilantro.

Nutrition

Calories: 186kcal | Protein: 3g | Fat: 8g | Fiber: 7g | Iron: 1mg

CREAMY VEGETABLE SOUP

PREP TIME: 20 MINS COOK TIME: 40 MINS TOTAL TIME: 1 HOUR
YIELD: 6 TO 8 SERVINGS

Ingredients

- One medium sweet potato (approximately one pound), peeled and diced; one yellow squash or zucchini; one small head of cauliflower; one medium white onion; one red bell pepper; two tablespoons olive oil; and freshly cracked black pepper
- four minced garlic cloves
- two to three cups of vegetable stock
- One fifteen-oz can of coconut milk
- One fifteen-oz can of fire-roasted tomatoes.
- One fifteen-ounce bag of washed and drained white beans
- One teaspoon of cumin powder
- One tsp of smoky paprika

Instructions

1. Prepare the oven. Preheat the oven to 425°F.
2. Roasting the vegetables will bring out their natural flavours and create a delicious side dish. Arrange the bell pepper, sweet potato, yellow squash, cauliflower, and white onion on a spacious sheet pan. Coat evenly by drizzling with 1 1/2 tablespoons of olive oil and tossing. Distribute the vegetables evenly and season them generously with salt and pepper. Cook for 30 to 40 minutes, or until tender and slightly blackened.
3. Cook gently. After the veggies have been baking for about 20 minutes, it's time to heat up the remaining olive oil in a large stockpot over medium-high heat. Sauté the garlic for 1-2 minutes, stirring occasionally, until it becomes fragrant. Incorporate the vegetable broth, coconut milk, tomatoes, white beans, cumin, and smoked paprika, ensuring they are well mixed. Keep cooking until the mixture is gently simmering. (Then, if the vegetables are not cooked yet, you can cover the dish and lower the heat to a gentle simmer. Otherwise, continue.
4. Blend. Incorporate the roasted vegetables into the soup and gently mix them together. Blend the soup until it reaches a smooth consistency using an immersion blender.
5. Flavor. Adjust the seasoning of the soup with salt and pepper to your liking. If you'd like a lighter consistency, feel free to incorporate additional vegetable broth.
6. Present. Enjoy your dish by serving it warm, with a swirl of extra coconut milk and a twist of black pepper if you like.

BLUEBERRY SMOOTHIE

PREP TIME: 5 MINS TOTAL TIME: 5 MINS

Ingredients

- One cup of fresh or frozen blueberries
- One eight-oz carton of plain yogurt
- ¾ cup 2% low-fat milk
- Two tsp of white sugar
- One-half teaspoon of vanilla extract
- One-third teaspoon ground nutmeg

Directions

1. Mix together blueberries, yoghurt, milk, sugar, vanilla, and nutmeg in a blender until the mixture becomes frothy. Make sure to scrape down the sides of the blender if necessary.
2. Divide the mixture evenly into two glasses and serve right away.

AWESOME BROCCOLI CHEESE SOUP

TOTAL TIME: 45 MINUTES YIELD: 4–6 SERVINGS

Ingredients

- Five tablespoons of butter, separated
- One little onion, finely chopped
- three minced garlic cloves
- 1 cup finely chopped broccoli stems (optional)
- 1/4 cup of flour for all purposes
- one cup of whole milk
- One cup of half-and-half
- 2 Half a cup of vegetable or chicken broth
- Two to three cups of finely chopped broccoli florets
- One large carrot, cut thinly
- One teaspoon salt, added to taste.
- half a teaspoon of finely powdered black pepper
- Half a teaspoon of paprika and an 8-ounce grated block of premium extra-sharp cheddar cheese

Instructions

1. Begin by sautéing garlic and onion. Take a large soup pot or Dutch oven and melt 1 tablespoon of butter over medium heat. Sauté the onion, garlic, and broccoli stems until they become soft and release a delightful aroma, which usually takes around 5 minutes.
2. Create your roux: Incorporate the remaining 4 tablespoons of butter into the soup pot. Once the butter has melted, go ahead and add the flour to the pot. Simmer gently over medium heat for approximately 2-3 minutes, until the flour has thickened. Gradually add the milk and half and half while whisking continuously. (It will begin with a rich consistency, but over time it will become more velvety and reminiscent of a smooth soup base.) Keep thinning it out, slowly whisking in the broth. Cook for about 10 minutes, stirring occasionally to blend in any skin that may develop.
3. Include broccoli: Once the soup base has reached a thick consistency, gently incorporate the broccoli, carrots, and a blend of aromatic spices. Cook for about 10 minutes, until the broccoli pieces are vibrant green and tender when pierced with a fork.
4. Include cheese: Remove the pot from the heat and let it cool for a few minutes. Incorporate the majority of the cheese until it has fully melted. Present the dish in bowls, accompanied by a generous sprinkle of additional cheese and a slice of crusty bread for dipping. Feel free to indulge in the comforting delight of this meal, allowing yourself to experience a wave of cosy emotions. This is a joyous occasion!

BROCCOLI CHEDDAR SOUP

PREP TIME: 10MINUTES COOK TIME: 25MINUTES TOTAL TIME: 35MINUTES SERVES 4

Ingredients

- Four tsp unsalted butter
- ½ teaspoon sea salt and one medium yellow onion, sliced
- freshly ground black pepper
- Three chopped garlic cloves and ¼ cup all-purpose flour
- Two cups of unsweetened almond milk or whole milk
- two cups of broth made of vegetables
- Chopped broccoli florets in three cups
- One large carrot, cut finely or julienned
- One-half tsp Dijon mustard
- Eight ounces (about two generous cups) of shredded cheddar cheese
- Optional: homemade croutons for serving

Instructions

1. Heat the butter in a spacious pot or Dutch oven on medium heat. Sauté the onion with a pinch of salt and a few twists of pepper, stirring constantly, until it becomes tender, about 5 minutes. Incorporate the garlic into the mixture and continue cooking for an additional minute. Next, add the flour and vigorously whisk for 1 to 2 minutes, until the flour takes on a golden hue. Add the milk gradually while whisking constantly.
2. Mix in the broth, broccoli, carrot, and mustard until well combined. Cook for 15 to 20 minutes or until the broccoli is tender.
3. Slowly incorporate the cheese, giving it a good stir after each addition, until it's fully melted and the soup reaches a smooth, creamy consistency. Adjust the seasoning according to your preference and, if you like, add some croutons for extra flavour.

MINESTRONE SOUP

PREP TIME: 15MINUTES COOK TIME: 30MINUTES SERVES 4 TO 6

Equipment

Staub Dutch Oven

Ingredients

- Two tablespoons of pure olive oil
- One medium yellow onion, minced; two medium carrots; two thinly sliced celery ribs
- One tsp sea salt and more to taste
- freshly ground black pepper
- 3 grated garlic cloves
- One 28-oz can of chopped tomatoes
- 1 1/2 cups cooked, drained, and rinsed kidney or white beans
- one cup of finely chopped green beans
- Four cups of veggie broth and two bay leaves
- One tsp of dehydrated oregano
- A single tsp of dried thyme
- shells, orecchiette, elbows, and 3/4 cup tiny pasta
- ½ cup of freshly chopped parsley
- A few pinches of red chili flakes
- Optional: grated Parmesan cheese for presentation

Instructions

1. Warm up the oil in a spacious pot on a medium heat setting. Incorporate the onion, carrots, celery, salt, and a few twists of black pepper into the mixture, and continue to cook, stirring occasionally, for 8 minutes until the vegetables start to become tender.
2. Incorporate the garlic, tomatoes, beans, green beans, broth, bay leaves, oregano, and thyme. Allow to cook gently for 20 minutes.
3. Add the pasta to the mixture and continue cooking for an additional 10 minutes until the pasta is fully cooked.
4. Adjust the seasoning according to your preference and garnish with parsley, red pepper flakes, and parmesan, if you like.

EASY BLUEBERRY OATMEAL

PREP TIME: 2 MINUTES COOK TIME: 10 MINUTES YIELD: 2

Ingredients

- One tablespoon of coconut oil or salted butter
- One cup of traditional rolled oats (do not use steel-cut or quick oats)
- one cup of water
- ½ cup 2% or oat milk, depending on preference
- One cup of frozen or fresh blueberries
- Two tsp of brown sugar
- One-half teaspoon of cinnamon
- One-half teaspoon of allspice
- 1/4 tsp kosher salt
- One-half teaspoon of vanilla extract
- Maple syrup, milk, sliced almonds, and fresh blueberries are used as toppings.

Instructions

1. Heat the butter or coconut oil in a saucepan over medium heat until melted. Toast the oats for approximately 2 to 3 minutes, stirring frequently, until they become fragrant.
2. Lower the heat and gently add the water, milk, blueberries, brown sugar, cinnamon, allspice, salt, and vanilla extract, stirring carefully. Simmer the mixture for 5 to 7 minutes until it thickens and the oats become tender. While stirring, gently crush the blueberries with the back of a spoon. Make sure to crush most of the berries to give the oatmeal a vibrant purple hue.
3. Take it off the heat. Finish off with your favourite toppings and serve.

Notes

1. When using frozen blueberries, it's important to be mindful of their tendency to bleed their color, as this can be less than ideal for baked goods. However, if you're looking for a delightful twist to your oatmeal, using frozen berries is a great option! No need to thaw them beforehand. The heat of the pan will defrost them in no time.

CHICKEN NOODLE SOUP

PREP: 10 MINS COOK: 30 MINSSERVES 2

Ingredients

- 900ml Miso soup mix or chicken or veggie stock
- One skinless, boneless (175g) chicken breast
- 1 tsp freshly sliced ginger
- One freshly minced garlic clove, fifty grams of rice or wheat noodles
- 2 tablespoons frozen or canned sweetcorn
- two to three tiny-sliced mushrooms
- Two shredded spring onions, two tsp soy sauce, plus enough to serve
- To serve, add some shredded chilli and optional mint or basil leaves.

Instructions

1. Add the stock to a pan and combine it with the chicken breast, ginger, and garlic. Bring the mixture to a boil, then lower the heat, partially cover, and let it simmer for 20 minutes until the chicken becomes tender.
2. Place the chicken on a cutting board and delicately pull it apart into small, manageable pieces using two forks. Add the chicken back into the stock along with the noodles, sweetcorn, mushrooms, spring onion, and a drizzle of soy sauce. Cook for 3-4 minutes until the noodles are tender.
3. Serve the dish by dividing it into two bowls and garnishing with the remaining spring onion, mint or basil leaves, and chili, if desired. Don't forget to add a generous drizzle of soy sauce for an extra burst of flavour.

BUTTERNUT SQUASH SOUP

PREP TIME: 20 MINS COOK TIME: 45 MINS TOTAL TIME: 1 HR 5 MINS

Ingredients

- two tsp butter
- One medium butternut squash, peeled, seeded, and cubed;
- one small onion;
- one stalk celery;
- one medium carrot;
- two medium potatoes;
- one (32 fluid ounce) container chicken stock; salt and freshly ground black pepper to taste

Directions

1. Collect all the necessary ingredients.
2. Warm up the butter in a spacious pot on medium heat, and sauté the onion, celery, carrot, potatoes, and squash until they develop a light golden colour, which should take around 5 minutes. Add chicken stock until the vegetables are completely covered.
3. Heat the mixture until it reaches a boiling point. Lower the heat and cover the pot, allowing the vegetables to simmer until they are tender, which should take around 40 minutes.
4. Puree the soup in a blender until it reaches a smooth consistency. Finish by returning to the pot and incorporating any remaining stock until you achieve your desired consistency. Add a dash of salt and pepper for the perfect seasoning.
5. Indulge in the deliciousness while it's still piping hot!

EASY BROCCOLI CHEESE SOUP

PREP: 5 MINUTES COOK: 25 MINUTES TOTAL: 30 MINUTES

Ingredients

- tbsp (15g) olive oil or butter
- two minced cloves of garlic
- One chopped onion (brown, white, yellow)
- Four cups (one liter) of low-sodium chicken broth or stock
- 325ml, or 1.5 cups, of water
- Broccoli florets, 700g / 1.4lb (2 large broccoli plus sliced peeled stem

- Two potatoes, peeled and cut into cubes about 1.5 cm / 2/3 "
- 3/4 teaspoon salt
- 1/4 teaspoon ground pepper
- 1.5cups (150g) of shredded cheddar cheese (or your preferred cheese)
- 3/4 cup (165 ml) milk or cream

To Serve (Optional)

- Cream, for drizzling
- Extra grated cheese

Instructions

2. Heat up some butter in a large pot over medium-high heat. Sauté the onion and garlic until they are softened, which should take about 2 minutes.
3. Include some broth or water, along with broccoli, potato, and a pinch of salt and pepper. Simmer the mixture until the lid can be placed on top. Reduce the heat to medium high and let it cook for about 20 minutes, or until the broccoli becomes tender.
4. Remember to turn off the stove, but leave it on the stove. Blend until smooth using a stick blender.
5. Incorporate the cream into the mixture, gradually adding the cheese and stirring consistently to ensure it melts smoothly.
6. Adjust the seasoning to your liking by adding more salt if needed.
7. Serve the dish in bowls. Add a touch of cream and sprinkle some extra grated cheese on top, if you'd like.

Recipe Notes:

1. Broccoli - Begin by separating the florets and removing the tough skin from the stem. Proceed to dice the stem into small pieces before adding them to the pot.
2. When you work with two large broccoli heads, you'll end up with approximately 700g/1.4lb of delicious broccoli, stems included. Frozen broccoli can also be used.
3. When pureeing soup, it's important to take precautions to avoid any messy mishaps. If you're using a blender, it's best to blend the soup in two batches and let it cool down a bit before blitzing. This way, you can prevent any potential soup explosions that might occur if you blend hot soup in a fully sealed blender. Safety first! Put the lid on the blender, but take off the lid for the feeding hole. Place a folded tea towel over the hole and secure it with your hand. Begin at a low setting and gradually increase the speed.
4. Storage - the dish can be refrigerated for 4 to 5 days without any issues, and it freezes exceptionally well for several months
5. Dietary information for each portion. Can be made with full fat milk instead of cream to reduce the calorie count to 280.

CHAPTER 6: SOLID FOOD RECIPES

COUNTRY STYLE GRAVY MEATBALLS

PREP TIME30MINUTES COOK TIME30MINUTES TOTAL TIME1HOUR

Ingredients

- 32 ounces of pork sausage in bulk
- 1 cup breadcrumbs from Panko
- One medium-sized onion, or ½ cup of sliced yellow onion,
- ½ cup of freshly chopped parsley
- Two big eggs
- Two tsp black pepper, separated
- 1½ tsp salt, separated
- two tsp butter
- One tablespoon bacon drippings
- Two teaspoons of unbleached all-purpose flour
- 1/4 cup 2% milk

Instructions

Make the meatballs:

1. Set the oven temperature to 375° F. Prepare a large baking sheet by lining it with parchment paper or foil.
2. Mix together the pork sausage, breadcrumbs, onion, parsley, eggs, black pepper, and salt in a large bowl. Ensure that the ingredients are thoroughly combined, and if the mixture appears to be lacking moisture, consider adding a tablespoon or two of water.
3. Shape the sausage mixture into 1½ inch balls (a spring-loaded scoop works well) and arrange them on the prepared baking sheet. Ensure that there is a consistent and uniform spacing of approximately one inch between each item.
4. Ensure that the meatballs are perfectly cooked by baking them for 25-30 minutes. They should reach an internal temperature of 160 degrees F and have no traces of pink left.

While the meatballs are cooking, make the cream gravy:

1. Combine the butter and bacon drippings in a saucepan and gently heat until melted. Combine the flour, remaining black pepper, and the remaining salt with the butter, stirring until well mixed.
2. Heat the mixture over medium heat for about a minute, stirring continuously. Add the milk and mix everything together.

3. Keep cooking the mixture, stirring consistently until it reaches a simmer. Reduce the heat slightly and stir the mixture for a minute or two. It will thicken rapidly once it starts simmering. After it thickens, take the pan off the heat.
4. Give the gravy a taste and adjust the seasoning with a touch of salt or pepper if desired. Just be mindful not to overdo it, as the meatballs already contain some salt.
5. Once the meatballs are cooked to perfection, delicately transfer them onto a beautiful serving platter using tongs. Drizzle the steaming gravy over the meatballs and serve them right away.

To serve them as an appetizer:

Place the tongs conveniently beside the platter of delicious meatballs and savoury gravy, allowing guests to help themselves. Please ensure that forks or toothpicks are available.

To serve them as part of a meal:

1. The meatballs and gravy are absolutely scrumptious when served over biscuits for a classic breakfast. Divide the biscuits in half and place them on the plates. Arrange the meatballs and gravy on top of the halves.
2. When it comes to a delightful dinner dish, there's nothing quite like the harmonious blend of tender meatballs and rich gravy. Pair it with some freshly cooked egg noodles or other pasta, or even serve it over a bed of fluffy cooked rice. The possibilities are endless!
3. Produces approximately 48 meatballs and 1½ cups of savoury gravy.

Nutrition

Calories: 453kcal Fiber: 1g Sugar: 3g Vitamin A: 601IU Vitamin C: 7mg Calcium: 94mg Iron: 2mg

TURKEY MEATLOAF

PREP TIME: 10MINUTES COOK TIME: 45MINUTES TOTAL TIME: 55MINUTES

Ingredients
Meatloaf:

- One pound of ground beef and one pound of ground turkey, or two pounds of 90% lean ground turkey
- Pork breadcrumbs, ½ cup
- 1/4 cup of whole milk or beef broth, with additional as necessary
- Two giant, whisked eggs

- Two teaspoons of dried parsley or two tablespoons of fresh parsley
- Two tsp Worcestershire sauce
- Half a teaspoon of ketchup
- One-half tsp Kosher salt and one-half tsp ground black pepper
- one tsp powdered garlic
- One tsp powdered onion

Sauce:

- ½ cup of BBQ sauce or ketchup; I use a half-and-half mixture.
- Twice as much light brown sugar

Instructions

1. Set the oven temperature to 375°F. Prepare a baking sheet or a 9×5-inch loaf pan by lining it with foil. Give it a light spritz of nonstick spray and set it aside.
2. Combine the turkey, breadcrumbs, milk, eggs, parsley, Worcestershire sauce, ketchup, salt, pepper, garlic powder, and onion powder in a large bowl. Be careful not to mix too much, as it may affect the tenderness of the meat.
3. Shape the mixture into a loaf on the baking sheet. Combine the ketchup and/or BBQ sauce with brown sugar in a small bowl. Drizzle the mixture on top of the meatloaf. Feel free to sprinkle some pepper on top if you'd like.
4. Cook the meatloaf for 45 to 55 minutes, or until the center reaches a temperature of 160°F. Let it rest for 5 to 10 minutes before cutting it into 8 to 10 slices.

Notes
Variations:

1. Feel free to use fresh onion and garlic instead (1/2 cup onion, 4 garlic cloves minced). Just remember to sauté them with a touch of olive oil before adding them to the meat.
2. If you enjoy a bit of spiciness, consider incorporating a touch of red pepper flakes into the meat or a few dashes of chilli sauce or sriracha into the meatloaf sauce.
3. If you're looking to create a gluten-free version, consider using gluten-free bread crumbs or old-fashioned oats.
4. If you're a fan of a saucier meatloaf, feel free to whip up an additional batch and generously brush it on during the final 10 minutes of cooking. You can even use it as a delectable dipping sauce!
5. Remember to choose high-quality ground turkey for the best flavor.

Nutrition

Calories: 244kcal | Protein: 24g | Fat: 11g | Fiber: 1g | Sugar: 8g | Iron: 2mg

AVOCADO SCRAMBLED EGGS

PREP TIME: 3MINUTES COOK TIME: 5MINUTES TOTAL TIME: 8MINUTES SERVINGS: 1 SERVING

Ingredients

- Two big eggs
- One tablespoon of butter without salt
- half an avocado
- To taste, add flake salt.
- To taste, grind black pepper
- Optional: shredded cheddar cheese

Instructions

1. Combine two eggs in a bowl and whisk until well mixed.
2. Warm up a non-stick skillet on a gentle flame. Incorporate the butter and allow it to slowly melt. After the butter has melted, gently introduce the egg into the pan and let it rest for a minimum of 20 seconds.
3. With a spatula, gently lift the egg and fold it over twice. Let it cook for 10 seconds. Incorporate the avocado and cheese (if desired) and fold once more. Prepare the dish for a brief moment.
4. Take off the heat and allow it to rest for a few seconds. Season with flake salt and ground pepper. Ensure the dish is served at its optimal temperature.

Nutrition

Calories: 423kcal | Carbohydrates: 9g | Protein: 16g | Fiber: 7g | Sugar: 1g

ROASTED VEGETABLE PUREE

PREP TIME: 10MINUTES COOK TIME: 1HOUR TOTAL TIME: 1HOUR 10MINUTES SERVINGS: 8 CUPS

Ingredients

- Two pounds of summer squash or other mixed veggies, like zucchini, tomatoes, eggplant, peppers, onions, and carrots
- using olive oil to drizzle freshly ground pepper and kosher salt
- three-cup water cloves chopped and peeled garlic bay leaf

Instructions

1. Set the oven to 400 degrees.
2. Vegetables should be cut in half and arranged in a single layer on the sheet pan.
3. One pound of summer squash
4. Add a liberal amount of salt and pepper, then drizzle with the olive oil.
5. freshly ground pepper, kosher salt, and olive oil for drizzling
6. Roast until very soft and beginning to brown, 30 to 45 minutes.
7. Put the veggies in a big saucepan. If using, remove the flesh from the eggplant and throw away the peels. If using peppers, remove the skins and throw them away. Add the bay leaf, garlic, and water.
8. 3 cups water, bay leaf, cloves of garlic,
9. Simmer until the vegetables are very soft, about 20 minutes.
10. Smoothly mix with an immersion blender.
11. Can be frozen and chilled for later use.

Notes

1. Swap out tomato sauce for a flavorful vegetable puree in your recipes. The taste will differ based on the vegetables and the dish they are incorporated into.
2. Ensure that any remaining food is properly stored in a sealed container and placed in the refrigerator within a reasonable timeframe, typically no longer than 3 days. Store your food in the freezer in 1- or 2-cup portions to keep it fresh for longer. Thaw and incorporate into your recipes.
3. Estimated nutritional values are provided for a serving size of 1 cup.

Nutrition

Calories: 18kcal | Carbohydrates: 4g | Protein: 1g | Sugar: 2g | Calcium: 20mg | Iron: 1mg

CHICKEN AND RICE CASSEROLE

PREP TIME10MINUTES COOK TIME2HOURS TOTAL TIME2HOURS 10MINUTES MINS

Ingredients

- 1 1/2 cups long-grain white rice
- Two cans of homemade or commercially available cream of mushroom or chicken soup
- one cup of water
- two glasses of milk
- One package of Lipton's onion soup mix or one batch of homemade onion soup mix

- One and a half cups of shredded cheddar cheese, divided among three thick, skinless, boneless chicken breasts or thighs, along with freshly ground black pepper and salt

Instructions

1. Set the oven temperature to 350 degrees F. Prepare a 9x13" pan (or a casserole dish of similar size) by applying a light coating of non-stick cooking spray. Put it aside.
2. Mix together rice, cream of soups, milk, water, and onion soup seasoning in a bowl until well combined. Transfer the mixture into the pan that has been prepared. Add a generous layer of the shredded cheddar cheese.
3. Place the chicken breasts gently into the rice mixture. Be sure to cover the dish with aluminum foil (the pan will be very full!) and bake it for 1 hour 30 minutes to 2 hours. This will ensure that the rice becomes tender and the chicken is thoroughly cooked. (Typically, the baking time is around 1.5 hours, although it can be influenced by factors such as oven type, altitude, and other variables).
4. Take out of the oven and generously sprinkle the remaining cheese over the dish. Let it cool for 15-20 minutes before serving.
5. Pair it with a side of freshly steamed vegetables or a crisp green salad.

Notes

- Consider omitting the cheese or trying alternatives like Colby jack, mozzarella, or Swiss.
- Attention: Minute rice is not suitable for this recipe. If you opt for brown rice, it's important to note that it will need more liquid (at least 1/2 cup) and a longer cooking time. To prevent the chicken from overcooking or drying out, I recommend using chicken thighs instead of breasts.
- Enhance the taste of your dish by incorporating some fresh thyme, parsley, minced garlic, or a sprinkle of fresh basil.
- For a delicious twist to your casserole, consider adding some chopped broccoli florets before baking. It will add a burst of freshness and vibrant colour to your dish.
- Vegetables: You have the option to include some delicious additions like mushrooms, onions, green peppers, green beans, broccoli, and more.
- Cream of soup: My homemade version is incredibly simple and absolutely delightful, but feel free to use any variety of cream of soup for these recipes, such as chicken, mushroom, or celery.
- For the Instant Pot Chicken and Rice recipe, adjust the amount of water to 1/2 cup and milk to 1 cup. It is recommended to use only one can of cream of soup. Set the cooking time to 8-10 minutes, adjusting as needed for the thickness of the chicken breasts. Let it naturally release for 10 minutes.

- Prepare in advance Directions: Get the meal ready, but avoid putting it in the oven. Make sure to cover it thoroughly and place it in the refrigerator for 1-2 days prior to baking.
- Chilled Directions: Get the dish ready, but avoid putting it in the oven. Make sure to tightly cover it with plastic wrap and tinfoil before placing it in the freezer. It will stay fresh for up to 3 months. Make sure to let it thaw overnight in the refrigerator before baking uncovered.

Nutrition

Calories: 418kcal | Protein: 21g | Fat: 15g | Sugar: 4g | Calcium: 265mg | Iron: 1.5mg

CHICKEN AND RICE CASSEROLE

PREP TIME 10MINUTES COOK TIME 25MINUTES TOTAL TIME 35MINUTES YIELD 8 SERVINGS

Ingredients

- Three cups of cooked, shredded, or cubed chicken
- three cups of boiled rice
- Two 10.5-ounce cans of cream of chicken soup (or cream of potato or mushroom soup) equals twenty-one ounces.
- One tsp salt
- ½ teaspoon of black pepper, ground
- one-half teaspoon of paprika
- One-half teaspoon of powdered onion
- Half a teaspoon of powdered garlic
- two cups of frozen peas
- Split two cups of cheddar cheese shreds

Instructions

1. Set the oven temperature to 350°F.
2. Combine chicken, rice, soup, spices, peas, and 1 cup of shredded cheese in a large bowl. Spread the mixture evenly in a 9×13-inch casserole dish. Finish by adding the rest of the cheese on top.
3. Cook until thoroughly heated, approximately 20-30 minutes.

SWEET POTATO BLACK BEAN BOWLS

PREP: 15MINUTES COOK: 30MINUTES REST TIME FOR KALE: 30MINUTES

TOTAL: 1HOUR 15MINUTES

Ingredients

For The Kale:

- Two cups of chopped and de-stemmed kale
- Two tsp pure virgin olive oil
- 8 grammes of kosher salt

For The Roasted Sweet Potatoes:

- Peel and quarter four medium sweet potatoes lengthwise (total of 28 ounces peeled).
- Two tablespoons of pure olive oil
- One tsp of kosher salt
- One tsp of chili powder
- One tsp powdered chipotle
- One teaspoon of cumin powder
- 1/4 teaspoon of coriander powder
- One-half teaspoon of powdered garlic

For The Creamy Chipotle Sauce:

- One cup of dairy-free or vegan yogurt, or plain Greek yogurt with no added sugar
- In one chipotle pepper sauce
- Lime juice, two tablespoons
- two peeled garlic cloves
- salt that is kosher

For The Bowls:

- One fifteen-ounce can of rinsed and drained black beans
- two cups of brown rice, cooked
- One small avocado, pitted, peeled, and diced, yields four ounces.
- One cup of rapidly pickled red onions
- One cup of raw cilantro leaves
- Cut one lime into wedges.

Instructions

Prepare the kale:

1. Combine the kale, olive oil, and salt in a bowl. Gently massage the kale for 1 minute. The volume will decrease.
2. Allow it to sit at room temperature while preparing the remaining ingredients.

Prepare the sweet potatoes:

1. Ensure that the oven is preheated to 400°F and that the rack is positioned in the center of the oven.
2. As the oven preheats, you'll want to take those peeled and quartered sweet potatoes and place them in a large saucepan, making sure to cover them with water.
3. Heat until it reaches a boiling point. Cook the sweet potatoes until the edges are slightly tender when pressed with a fork, which should take around 8 minutes. It's important to avoid overcooking them, as that could result in a mushy texture.
4. After draining the sweet potatoes, gently pat them dry with a paper towel and proceed to cut them into bite-sized pieces.
5. Combine the sweet potatoes with 2 tablespoons of the olive oil in a large bowl.
6. Combine the salt, chili powder, chipotle powder, cumin, coriander, and garlic powder in a small bowl.
7. Add the spice blend to the sweet potatoes and gently mix until they are evenly coated.
8. Spread out the sweet potatoes on a sheet pan and let them roast for 15 to 20 minutes. Remember to flip them once halfway through so they can become nicely browned and tender when pierced with a fork.

Make the creamy chipotle sauce:

1. Combine the yogurt, chipotle pepper, lime juice, garlic cloves, and a pinch of salt in a blender or small food processor. Puree until velvety and creamy.
2. Adjust the seasoning with salt according to your preference. Keep it aside until you're ready to put together the bowls, or you can store it in the refrigerator.

Assemble the bowls:

1. Arrange the kale, roasted sweet potatoes, black beans, brown rice, and avocado in serving bowls.
2. Add a finishing touch with the pickled red onions, creamy chipotle sauce, and cilantro. Don't forget to add a refreshing touch with some lime wedges.

Nutrition

Calories: 585 kcal, Protein: 20 g, Fiber: 21 g, Sugar: 13.5 g

BEEF STROGANOFF

PREP: 15MINUTES COOK: 15MINUTES TOTAL: 30MINUTES

Ingredients

- 600 g / 1.2 lb boneless rib eye or scotch fillet steak
- Two tablespoons vegetable oil, split; one large onion (or two small onions); 300 grammes / ten ounces of thinly sliced mushrooms
- 40g/3 tablespoons of butter
- Two tablespoons of flour
- Two cups (500 ml) of beef broth, ideally decreased in salt
- One tablespoon 150 ml / 2/3 cup sour cream Dijon mustard
- Add pepper and salt.

Serving:

- 250–300 g / 8–10 oz of preferred egg noodles or spaghetti
- Finely chopped chives, optional garnish

Instructions

1. Gently flatten the steaks to a thickness of about 3/4cm / 1/3" using a fist, rolling pin, or mallet. Cut the strips into 5mm / 1/5" slices, making sure to remove any excess fat.
2. Add a touch of salt and pepper.
3. Warm up 1 tbsp of oil in a spacious skillet on high heat. Distribute half of the beef in the skillet and swiftly spread it using tongs. Allow to sit undisturbed for 30 seconds until a golden brown color develops. Make sure to sear the beef swiftly (if possible!). Allow to sit undisturbed for 30 seconds to achieve a golden brown color. Transfer the dish to a plate right away. Rest assured, there is no need to be concerned about any pink bits or the possibility of it being undercooked.
4. Drizzle the remaining tablespoon of oil and repeat the process with the rest of the beef.
5. Lower the heat to a medium-high setting. Melt the butter. Next, sauté some onions for a minute before incorporating the mushrooms.
6. Ensure the mushrooms are cooked until they reach a delightful golden hue. Make sure to scrape the bottom of the fry pan to capture all those delicious golden bits, as they add incredible flavor to your dish.
7. Combine the flour and cook while stirring for 1 minute.
8. Incorporate half of the broth into the mixture while gently stirring. After it's been incorporated, go ahead and add the rest of the broth.

9. Mix the ingredients together, followed by the addition of sour cream and mustard. Continue stirring until everything is well combined. Even if the mixture appears separated, the sour cream will blend in smoothly as it warms up.
10. Bring the mixture to a gentle simmer, then lower the heat to a medium-low setting. After it thickens to the consistency of pouring cream (3 - 5 minutes), you can adjust the salt and pepper to your liking.
11. Reintroduce the beef, along with its flavorful juices. Cook over low heat for 1 minute, then take off the stove right away. Serve the dish over pasta or egg noodles and add a sprinkle of chives for extra flavor, if you'd like.

Recipe Notes:

- Optimal choice for stroganoff - select a high-quality, fast-cooking cut of beef like boneless rib eye, also known as scotch fillet.
- Boneless sirloin and sirloin steak tips
- Beef tenderloin? I wouldn't recommend it. These cuts of meat include beef round steak (also known as topside), skirt, flat iron, and hanger.
- Another option is to use pork - pork stroganoff is a dish that can also be found in Russia.
- Enhance the tenderness of your beef - in case you don't have a high-quality steak, I suggest using a simple Chinese technique known as "velveting" to tenderize it. This experience will completely transform your life! Take a look at the user feedback in that recipe for validation
- Any type of flour will work for this recipe, but I personally prefer using plain white flour (all purpose). Alternatively, you can incorporate 1 tbsp of cornstarch or cornflour into the stroganoff sauce for a gluten-free option.
- Preference - I prefer pairing this dish with short pastas, as opposed to long pastas. More convenient to consume. It pairs perfectly with mashed potato, rice, polenta - any dish that's perfect for savoring every drop of delicious gravy!
- Adjusting sauce consistency: If you prefer a thinner sauce, simply add a touch of water. However, it's important to avoid over-simmering in an attempt to thicken it. Once the beef is added, it will overcook the meat.
- Proper storage is key to maintaining freshness. You can keep it in the fridge for 3 to 4 days or freeze it for later use. Make sure to thaw the beef completely before reheating it, and be cautious not to overcook it!
- Per serving, based on 5 servings (4 hearty servings or 5 sensible servings), pasta not included.

HONEY GLAZED CHICKEN WITH SWEET POTATO MASH

PREP TIME 10 MINUTES COOK TIME 20 MINUTES TOTAL TIME: 30 MINUTES

SERVINGS 2

Ingredients

- 500 g of trimmed and sliced chicken thighs
- Spoonful of ActiFry mild soy sauce
- Lemon juice, one ActiFry spoonful half a lemon
- We had some leftovers from roast dinner: 1 tablespoon runny honey, 200 grams of green beans, and 400 grams of sweet potato mash.

Instructions

1. Combine the honey, lemon, and soy sauce with the chicken in a bowl, ensuring that the chicken is thoroughly coated with the marinade.
2. Transfer the mixture from the bowl to your ActiFry, ensuring that it is evenly distributed in the cooking pan. Set the timer for 18 minutes and let it cook.
3. Boil the beans in a pan of water for 4 minutes.
4. Warm up the mash in a bowl (covered) in the microwave for 5 minutes, remembering to give it a stir halfway through.
5. Present your culinary creation on a plate and savour every bite!

Recipe Notes

- If you don't happen to have any leftover mash, simply allocate some extra time to prepare a fresh batch! I enjoy sweet potato mash because it cooks more quickly than regular potatoes!
- The Honey Glazed Chicken was absolutely delightful, with a cooking process that ensured it remained moist and tender. The end result was a delectably sticky sauce that perfectly complemented the chicken. Well, this outcome is quite unexpected. Usually, it doesn't turn out like this when I prepare it in the oven! The dish turned out to be even more delectable and satisfying. I will certainly be preparing this recipe again in the future.
- Tefal aims to demonstrate how the ActiFry can be a valuable addition to promoting a nutritious diet and overall well-being. The ActiFry was designed to help people break away from the habit of ordering takeout on Friday nights and provide them with a healthier, yet still delicious option. It's truly a remarkable product, capable of cooking a wide variety of dishes beyond just popular takeout favorites. It consistently delivers excellent results.

SOUTHWEST SHREDDED CHICKEN SALAD

PREP TIME: 20MINUTES   COOK TIME: 20MINUTES   TOTAL TIME: 40MINUTES   YIELD: 4

Ingredients

Southwest Chicken Salad

- 1-1.5 lbs. tenderloin of chicken
- ½ cup dried, rinsed, and drained black beans
- ¾ cup sliced red bell pepper and ½ cup washed, drained, and dried chickpeas
- ¾ cup of dry and drained whole kernel corn
- ¾ cup diced and cored cucumber
- 1 cup of finely chopped shallots
- ¼ cup finely diced jalapeño, ¼ cup chopped cilantro, tiny amount of shredded cheddar cheese, salt, pepper, and to taste

Chili Lime Yogurt Dressing

- ½ cup Greek yogurt (0%).
- two teaspoons freshly squeezed lime juice
- The optimum amount is two teaspoons of diced green chillies with juice from a can.
- One-half teaspoon of cumin
- One-half teaspoon of chili powder
- One-half teaspoon of powdered garlic
- One-half teaspoon of salt
- two tsp warm water

Optional Garnishes

- Two tablespoons of green onion, a small ½ avocado diced, one lime thinly sliced, and tortilla chips split into wedges

Equipment

- One saucepan of boiling chicken
- One colander
- One tiny mixing bowl for the dressing
- One sizable salad in a mixing bowl

Instructions

1. Prepare a pot of boiling water and gently place the chicken tenderloin into it. Ensure that the dish is cooked for 15-18 minutes or until the internal temperature reaches 165 degrees. Remove the water and let the chicken cool down.

2. For now, get a small mixing bowl and mix together the 0% Greek yogurt, freshly squeezed lime juice, diced green chilis (with the juice), garlic powder, cumin, chili powder, salt, and warm water. Mix thoroughly and set aside.
3. Next, prepare all the vegetables and herbs. For this recipe, gather some black beans, chickpeas, whole kernel corn, cucumber, red bell pepper, shallots, and jalapeno. Make sure to drain and rinse the beans and chickpeas, and dry the corn kernels. Dice the cucumber, red bell pepper, shallots, and jalapeno, removing the core, veins, and seeds as needed.

Assemble

1. After the chicken has cooled down, you can start shredding it into a large mixing bowl. You can use your hands or two forks for this task.
2. Now, incorporate the black beans, corn kernels, red bell pepper, chickpeas, cucumber, shallots, and jalapeno that you've prepared.
3. Include the finely chopped cilantro and the shredded cheddar cheese. Blend thoroughly. Ensure that all dishes are properly seasoned with a combination of salt and black pepper.
4. Add as much or as little chili lime yogurt dressing as you like. I utilized approximately half of it. Mix until all ingredients are thoroughly coated. Make sure to store any extra dressing in the refrigerator, covered, for three to four days.
5. Garnish with freshly chopped green onions and thinly sliced avocado. Pair it with some crispy tortilla chips and a squeeze of fresh lime for a delightful combination.

MEATBALLS IN TOMATO SAUCE

PREPARATION35 MIN COOKING55 MIN SERVINGS6

Ingredients

Tomato Sauce

- three chopped garlic cloves
- One bay leaf
- 1/4 teaspoon crushed red pepper
- Two tablespoons (30 milliliters) extra virgin olive oil
- One can (769 ml/28 oz). whole plum tomatoes

Meatballs

- two pieces of white sandwich bread
- 60 ml or 1/4 cup milk

- One pound (450 grams) 1 1/2 cups of ground veal (150 g) freshly shredded Parmigiano-Reggiano
- One egg
- One finely minced garlic clove
- Ten grams, or 1/4 cup minced parsley with flat leaves
- Half a teaspoon of salt
- 1/2 tsp of fennel powder
- 1/4 teaspoon of dry oregano
- 1/4 teaspoon crushed red pepper

Preparation
Tomato Sauce

1. Heat a sizable nonstick skillet over medium-high heat and gently brown the garlic, bay leaf, and red pepper flakes in the oil. After adding the tomatoes, simmer for half an hour. Using a potato masher, coarsely crush the tomatoes once they start to break down. Add pepper and salt for seasoning. Stay warm.

Meatballs

1. Meanwhile, in a food processor, pulse the bread until it reaches a crumb-like consistency. In a spacious bowl, allow the bread crumbs to absorb the milk for 5 minutes. Incorporate the remaining ingredients thoroughly by using your hands.
2. With hands lightly oiled, shape each meatball using 2 tbsp (30 ml) of the mixture.
3. Put the meatballs into the tomato sauce, cover them up, and let them cook for about 10 minutes on medium-low heat. Remember to turn them a few times while they're cooking. Uncover and cook for an additional 10 minutes or until fully cooked.
4. Pair the meatballs with blanched rapini, pasta, or fresh bread for a delightful combination.

GROUND BEEF STROGANOFF

PREP TIME: 10MINUTES COOK TIME: 25MINUTES TOTAL TIME: 35MINUTES

Ingredients

- One tablespoon of olive oil
- A pound of lean ground beef
- Diced half of a medium onion
- One pound of sliced mushrooms and two chopped garlic cloves
- two tablespoons all-purpose flour

- One cup beef stock and one cup heavy cream
- one-third cup sour cream
- One tablespoon Worcestershire sauce
- Half a teaspoon salt, or to taste
- Half a teaspoon of ground black pepper, or to taste

Instructions

1. Heat up a sturdy, deep pan over medium-high heat with some olive oil. Combine the ground beef and stir until it is thoroughly broken down into small pieces. Incorporate onions and freshly minced garlic. Cook until the onion becomes translucent and takes on a rich golden brown colour.
2. Include sliced mushrooms and saute for an additional 5 minutes.
3. Incorporate the flour by stirring it until it is fully mixed in. Make sure to incorporate any lumps that may form.
4. Incorporate 1 cup of beef broth, 1 cup of whipping cream, 1 tablespoon of Worcestershire sauce, 1/2 teaspoon of salt, and 1/2 teaspoon of black pepper, then gently bring the mixture to a simmer. Reduce the heat and let it simmer for approximately 5 minutes.
5. Take it off the heat and incorporate some sour cream. Mix the ingredients thoroughly and add seasoning as desired. Pair with your choice of noodles, rice, or potatoes for a delicious meal.

Nutrition

257kcal calories6g carbs16g protein19g fat

MEATBALLS & MASHED POTATOES

PREP TIME: 10MINUTES COOK TIME: 15MINUTES TOTAL TIME: 25MINUTES CALORIES: 517KCA

Ingredients

- 4 medium-sized diced potatoes
- One pound of ground beef
- Three teaspoons of breadcrumbs
- three tsp of milk
- one cup of water
- One packet of brown gravy mix
- two tsp butter

- half a cup of milk

Instructions

1. Prepare a generous amount of water in a large pot. Include the cubed potatoes and simmer until they are soft, which usually takes around 15 minutes.
2. Meanwhile, combine the breadcrumbs and milk in a bowl and let them soak until they form a paste.
3. Combine the ground beef with the paste and mix together thoroughly with your hands.
4. Create uniformly sized meatballs, approximately 1 1/4 inch in diameter, by firmly shaping the meat into compact balls.
5. Place the meatballs in a spacious skillet and set the heat to medium-high. Let them get a nice golden colour on one side before flipping them. Ensure that the balls are evenly browned on both sides. This process takes about 10 minutes.
6. Once the cooking is complete, take out the meatballs from the pan. Add water to the pan and whisk in the brown gravy mix. Simmer until slightly thickened.
7. Once the potatoes are done cooking, carefully remove the water. Combine the potatoes using a masher or hand mixer. Mix in the butter and milk until thoroughly blended.
8. Pair your meatballs with a generous serving of creamy mashed potatoes and rich gravy.

Nutrition

Calories: 517kcal | Carbohydrates: 34g | Protein: 27g | Fat: 30g | Fiber: 6g | Sugar: 3g | Vitamin C: 24mg | Calcium: 145mg | Iron: 9mg

CHAPTER 7: BEVERAGES RECIPES

STRAWBERRY BANANA SMOOTHIE

PREP TIME: 5 MINUTES COOK TIME: 3 MINUTES TOTAL TIME: 8 MINUTES

Ingredients

- 2 cups strawberries frozen
- 1 banana, fresh or frozen
- 1 cup milk or almond milk
- ½ cup plain yogurt

Instructions

1. Simply place the frozen fruit in the blender and add the rest of the ingredients.
2. Puree until velvety, incorporating more milk if necessary. Make sure to serve the dish right away.
3. Freeze any extra blended smoothie into convenient cubes for later.

Notes

For a thicker smoothie, add less milk.

Nutrition Information

Calories: 190 | Carbohydrates: 33g | Protein: 7g | Fat: 4g Fiber: 4g | Sugar: 23g | Iron: 0.7 mg

CHOCOLATE ALMOND MILK

PREP TIME: 10MINUTES COOK TIME: 0MINUTES TOTAL TIME: 10MINUTES

Equipment

- Vitamin
- Nut Milk Bag
- Fine Mesh Strainer

Ingredients

- One cup of almonds, soaked for up to twelve hours in water
- Five teaspoons of cacao powder
- Five tablespoons of maple syrup, or eight Medrol dates with pits

- three and a half cups water

Instructions

1. After soaking the almonds, make sure to thoroughly drain and rinse them. It is recommended to use fresh water (not the soaking water) when preparing this recipe.
2. Blend together the almonds, cacao powder, maple syrup, and water in a high-speed blender. Puree until perfectly velvety and luscious, for a solid minute.
3. Strain the chocolate milk mixture through a nut milk bag, ensuring that all the liquid is extracted and only the dry pulp is left behind. Don't let that almond pulp go to waste! Keep it aside for one of the delicious recipes shared in this post. Another option is to utilize a fine mesh strainer for removing the almond pulp, in case you lack a nut milk bag. Alternatively, you could experiment with cheesecloth.
4. Place the chocolate almond milk into a sealed container and refrigerate it to cool. For optimal results, it is recommended to thoroughly shake the container of homemade almond milk to ensure proper mixing before pouring.
5. This homemade milk can be stored in the fridge for up to 4 days, or you have the option to freeze any leftovers by pouring them into an ice cube tray. Store frozen cubes in an airtight container for up to 3 months to keep them fresh and ready to enhance your smoothies.

Notes

1. For the date-sweetened almond milk, opt for a strainer instead of a nut milk bag. This way, you can avoid the hassle of dealing with slimy pulp that won't easily pass through a fine-mesh bag. Another option is to start by blending the almonds and water until smooth. Then, strain the mixture through a nut milk bag before blending in the cacao powder and dates.

Nutrition

Calories: 287kcal, Carbohydrates: 28g, Protein: 9g Sugar: 16g, Calcium: 136mg, Iron: 2mg

CREAMY VANILLA MILKSHAKE

PREP TIME 2 MINUTES COOKING TIME 0 MINUTES SERVINGS 2 SERVINGS

Ingredients

- For the milkshake:
- Two cups of vanilla ice cream
- Half a cup of milk

- One-half tsp pure vanilla extract
- To Serve:
- Whipping cream as a garnish

Directions

1. Incorporate all the ingredients into a blender and blend until they are thoroughly mixed together.
2. Present the dish in elegant cups and garnish with a dollop of luscious whipped cream. Have a great time!

PINEAPPLE COCONUT WATER

SERVES 2 PREP TIME 5 MINS TOTAL TIME 5 MINS

Ingredients

- 180 ml or 3/4 cup of fresh pineapple juice
- 1/2 teaspoon of pure ginger juice and 1/2 cup (120 ml) of pure coconut water
- One lime; one teaspoon of runny honey, if necessary

Instructions

1. Mix together the pineapple juice, coconut water, and ginger juice in a cocktail shaker or Mason jar filled with ice. Make sure to give it a good shake, then give it a taste. If it needs a touch of sweetness, you can add a bit of honey. If the pineapple has a sufficient level of sweetness, there may not be a need for a significant amount of honey, if any at all.
2. Prepare small, chilled glasses with an abundance of ice cubes and delicate lime slices. Add the pineapple coconut water to the glasses, and for an extra touch, give it a squeeze of lime if desired.

APPLE CINNAMON SMOOTHIE

PREP TIME 10 minutes TOTAL TIME 10 minutes

Ingredients

- half a cup of your preferred milk
- half a cup of Greek yogurt, plain
- 1/3 cup of gluten-free rolled oats; peel, core, and cut 1 apple
- One large frozen banana, cut

- One spoonful of maple syrup
- One spoonful of butter made of almonds
- One tsp vanilla
- one and a half tsp ground cinnamon

Instructions

1. Blend all the ingredients together in a blender until they become smooth. Add a delightful touch to your smoothies by sprinkling them with a generous amount of cinnamon and garnishing with toasted walnuts or pecans, if you prefer.

BLUEBERRY ICED GREEN TEA

PREP TIME: 5 MINUTES COOK TIME: 5 MINUTES TOTAL TIME: 10 MINUTES SERVINGS: 8CUPS

Ingredients

- 8 cups water
- 4 green tea bags
- 1 cup blueberry syrup or to taste
- ice

Directions

1. Heat 2 cups of water until it reaches a boiling point, then take it off the heat.
2. Combine 1/2 cup of water at room temperature, then introduce the tea bags and allow them to steep for 10 minutes.
3. Take out the tea bags and pour in the rest of the water.
4. Incorporate the blueberry syrup until it reaches the desired level of sweetness.
5. Refrigerate, add ice, and savor the refreshing taste.

VANILLA CHAI LATTE

PREP TIME: 10 MINUTES COOK TIME: 0 MINUTES YIELD: 1 LARGE OR 2 SMALL

Ingredients

- One-tspn DIY Chai Spice Blend
- one cup of water
- One teaspoon of loose black tea leaves in a tea strainer, or one bag of black tea

- ½ cup of fresh whole or 2% milk* and 1 teaspoon of vanilla
- One tablespoon of pure maple syrup (or simple syrup, agave, or honey)

Instructions

1. Combine the chai spices, water, and tea bag in a small saucepan and heat over medium-high until it comes to a boil. After reaching a boiling point, take it off the heat and let it rest for a minute. After straining the mixture through a fine mesh strainer, pour it into one or two mugs - one for a large latte and two for small servings.
2. Give the saucepan a good rinse. Incorporate the milk, vanilla, and maple syrup. Heat the milk to 150 degrees Fahrenheit (measure using a thermometer): it should be hot with small bubbles forming around the outside, but not simmering. Precise temperature is crucial for achieving the ideal foam (in case you don't have a thermometer, you can make an estimation).
3. Try using a hand frothier, whisk, or French press to create a delightful foam with the milk. The French press is a popular choice for this method: Simply pour the hot milk into the French press and vigorously pump it until it becomes frothy. For 2% milk, this usually takes about 100 pumps or around 1 minute, while whole milk typically requires 50 pumps. Allow the foam to rest for approximately 30 seconds, giving it time to set.
4. Distribute the milk and foam evenly between the mugs (or into 1 mug). Enhance with extra chai spices and present.

Notes

When it comes to producing a good foam, fresh milk is the finest option. When you open a container of milk that has been sitting out for several days, you could discover that it no longer produces froth.

ORANGE CREAMSICLE SMOOTHIE

PREP: 5 COOK: 5 TOTAL: 10 MINUTES YIELD 3 SERVINGS

Ingredients

- One orange each, seeded and peeled
- One and a half cups of ice
- One can of coconut milk, the thick, white section only If the smoothie is thick, save the liquid to add.
- half a cup of Greek yogurt, plain
- Two tablespoons of honey
- Two tsp of vanilla essence

Instructions

1. Put the ingredients in the order that they are listed in a blender that has a lot of power.
2. Blend the ingredients until they are perfectly smooth, adding any more liquid from the bottom of the can of coconut milk if the mixture is too thick.

HOMEMADE SPORTS DRINK

Ingredients

- 8 cups fresh cold water, divided
- 3 tablespoons honey
- ½ teaspoon fine Himalayan pink salt
- ¾ teaspoon calcium magnesium powder (Optional)
- 1 pinch cayenne pepper
- ¾ cup freshly squeezed orange juice, strained
- 2 medium lemons, juiced
- 2 medium limes, juiced

Directions

1. Add 1 cup of water to a large pot. Include honey, salt, calcium magnesium powder, and cayenne in the mixture. Place the pot over a gentle heat and whisk until all the ingredients have completely dissolved. Take off the heat and let it cool down to room temperature.
2. Incorporate the juices into the mixture in the pot, which should be at room temperature. Add the remaining 7 cups of water and whisk until everything is well blended.

CREAMY COCONUT MILKSHAKE

PREP TIME: 5MINUTES COOK TIME: 0MINUTES TOTAL TIME: 5MINUTES SERVINGS: 1

Equipment

High-speed blender

Ingredients

- One medium-sized, ripe, frozen banana, peeled
- 30g per serving, one scoop Coconut or vanilla ice cream (dairy-free or standard)

- One cup of canned full-fat coconut milk

Instructions

1. Start by adding coconut milk to a high-speed blender, followed by the frozen banana and ice cream.
2. Puree until the mixture is velvety and free of any banana lumps. Ensure that the flavor and consistency are to your liking, making any necessary adjustments by adding more ice cream for sweetness or coconut milk to achieve the desired thickness.
3. It is recommended to serve the dish immediately in a glass and optionally garnish it with whipped cream.

Notes

- Vegan cooking creams like almond or soy creamer can be used in place of coconut milk. To achieve the same results as coconut milk, it's best to use a high-fat alternative.
- Storage in the Refrigerator: Although it is recommended to have this coconut milkshake as soon as it is prepared, it may also be kept in the refrigerator for up to twenty-four hours in a mason jar instead.
- It is possible to freeze the milkshake for up to three months if you pour it onto an ice cube tray and then freeze it. At the time when you are ready to drink the beverage, place the ice cubes in a high-speed blender and blend them until they are smooth and creamy. If necessary, add a small amount of milk or water to the mixture.

Nutrition

Serving: 1g | Calories: 574kcal | Carbohydrates: 45.3g | Protein: 5.6g Iron: 2mg

CARROT GINGER JUICE RECIPE

PREP IN 10 M COOKS IN 5 MTOTAL IN 15 M

Ingredients

- 4 Carrots (Gajjar), roughly diced
- 1 inch Ginger
- Lemon juice, from one lemon (optional)
- Honey, (optional)

Instructions

1. Adding the carrots and ginger to the juicer and then extracting the juice from them is the first step in the process of preparing the Carrot Ginger Juice Recipe.

2. Add a little more water, so we can extract more from the pulp of the carrot juice that remains in the juicer. Pour the juice into a jar and squeeze the juice from one lemon.
3. Add just the taste by adding salt or honey of required. You can also adjust the concentration of the juice by adding water or even squeezing some orange juice.
4. Serve the Carrot Ginger Juice as soon as it is made to get maximum benefits. Serve it with Grilled Sub Sandwich Recipes with Paneer & Roasted Vegetables for a healthy breakfast.

CREAMY MANGO LASSI

PREP TIME: 5MINUTES TOTAL TIME: 5MINUTES SERVINGS: 2 GLASSES
CALORIES: 212KCAL

Ingredients

- 1 ½ cups of cubed mangoes or 1 cup of mango pulp
- Half a cup of thick plain yogurt
- ¼ cup Water/Milk
- One spoonful of sugar
- Six to Eight Ice Cubes
- Sliced Pistachios as a garnish
- Strands of saffron (garnish)

Instructions

1. Make a smooth mixture by blending together the mango, yogurt, milk, and sugar with ice cubes. The mango lassi should be poured into two tall glasses, and then the pistachios and saffron strands should be mixed in as garnish. For serving, chill.

Notes

- Mango Lassi can be made vegan by: Replace the yogurt and milk with alternatives that do not contain dairy.
- To use fruit, either fresh or frozen: In the event that you are unable to obtain fresh fruit or pulp, you can use frozen fruit, which is readily accessible in shopping centers.

Nutrition

Calories: 212kcal | Carbohydrates: 39g | Protein: 5g | Fat: 4g | Iron: 15mg

CHAPTER 8: SNACK AND DESSERTS RECIPES

BANANA OATMEAL COOKIES

PREP TIME5MINUTES COOK TIME15MINUTES TOTAL TIME20MINUTES

Equipment

- measuring spoons
- measuring cups
- glass batter bowl
- spatula
- potato masher
- baking sheet
- Parchment Paper

Ingredients

- Three overripe bananas, or roughly ¼ cup of mashed banana,
- 2 TBS maple syrup (or honey)
- One egg
- 1 teaspoon of real vanilla extract
- a quarter cup of quick-cooking oats
- 1 teaspoon powdered cinnamon
- One-half teaspoon of fine sea salt
- ½ cup chocolate chips or additional toppings like as raisins, dried cranberries, or shredded coconut

Instructions

1. Set the oven temperature to 350 degrees F. Prepare two baking sheets by lining them with parchment paper and set them aside.
2. In a spacious mixing bowl, gently mash the bananas.
3. Combine honey, egg, and vanilla by stirring them together.
4. Mix in oats, cinnamon, and sea salt until well blended.
5. If you'd like, feel free to incorporate some additional ingredients and gently mix them in until they're well blended.
6. For precise measurements, you can use a 1 tablespoon measuring spoon or a 1 ½ TBS cookie scoop to portion out the dough. Make sure to place them on the baking sheet with a spacing of about 2" apart.
7. Place in the preheated oven for 12-15 minutes, or until the tops are perfectly set and the bottoms have a delicate hint of golden brown.

8. Allow the baked goods to cool on the baking sheet for 5 minutes, then transfer them to a wire cooling rack to cool completely.
9. It is best to serve the dish slightly warm or at room temperature.

To store/freeze:

- Ensure proper storage by placing the food in an airtight container. It can be kept at room temperature for 2 days, in the refrigerator for 5-7 days, or in the freezer for up to two months.

Ingredient Substitutions

- Those bananas that have seen better days. Ensure that your bananas are perfectly ripe and delightfully sweet. If you happen to have some frozen bananas on hand, make sure to thaw them either in the microwave or at room temperature before incorporating them into this recipe.
- Delicious sweeteners. Both liquid sweeteners are a great choice. Alternative sweeteners like agave or brown rice syrup are also viable options.
- Delicious and versatile, eggs are a staple ingredient in many culinary creations. You have the option of using a flax egg or egg replacer to create a vegan or egg-free version of these.
- Fast-cooking oats. Using rolled or old-fashioned oats will yield a slightly different texture.
- Delicious spice. Make sure to include it! These cookies are truly exceptional, thanks to the addition of cinnamon.
- Exquisite seasoning from the depths of the ocean. For optimal results, it is recommended to use half the amount of iodized salt.
- Indulge in the delightful goodness of chocolate chips. Both regular-sized and mini chips are perfect for this recipe. There are plenty of other options to consider: cinnamon chips, white chocolate chips, coconut, dried fruit like raisins, cherries, cranberries, blueberries, and more, peanut butter chips, chopped nuts, and so on.

Nutrition

Serving: 1cookie | Calories: 79kcal | Carbohydrates: 15g | Protein: 2g | Fat: 2g| Calcium: 1 3mg | Iron: 1mg

YOGURT PARFAIT

PREP TIME: 5 MINS TOTAL TIME: 5 MINS

Ingredients

- 2 cups vanilla yogurt
- 1 cup granola
- 8 blackberries

Directions

1. Arrange 1 cup of yogurt, 1/2 cup of granola, and 4 blackberries in a large glass, and then repeat the layers.

CHOCOLATE AVOCADO PUDDING

PREP TIME10 MINS TOTAL TIME10 MINS

Ingredients

- Using two ripe avocados without pits
- Four tsp unsweetened cocoa powder
- One tablespoon of optional hemp seeds
- Half a cup of milk; I like my vanilla almond milk unsweetened.
- Four tsp of pure maple syrup
- One tsp vanilla essence

Instructions

2. Mix together all the ingredients in a blender or food processor until they become smooth, making sure to scrape down the sides as needed. Feel free to add additional almond milk if necessary to achieve a smoother consistency.
3. Experiment with the flavors to find your desired taste. Adjust the amount of cocoa powder for a stronger chocolate flavor, add a touch of maple syrup for extra sweetness, or enhance the vanilla flavor. Puree until velvety.
4. Transfer to an airtight container for storage. Make sure to refrigerate the dish for a maximum of 4 days. Enjoy with a dollop of coconut whipped cream or any toppings you prefer, served chilled.

Notes

- Keep in mind that cacao powder has a stronger and better flavor compared to cocoa powder. So, if you decide to use it, you may need to add some extra sweetener to balance out the bitterness.
- Alternative sweeteners like honey or agave nectar can be used as well. I have a personal preference for maple syrup or date syrup. I haven't experimented with sugar-free syrups or stevia, but it should be successful as long as you're comfortable with the appropriate measurements.
- For optimal results, I suggest utilizing non-alcoholic vanilla flavoring. Using a moderate amount of vanilla extract is recommended to avoid any overpowering alcohol flavour. It's important to begin with a small amount and do some taste testing as you continue to add more, to prevent any unwanted outcomes.

Nutrition

Calories: 255kcal, carbohydrates: 25g, Protein: 4g

PEANUT BUTTER AND JELLY SMOOTHIE

PREP: 5MINUTES COOK: 0MINUTES TOTAL: 5MINUTES YIELD: 1 SERVING

SERVING SIZE: 1 SMOOTHIE

Equipment

Blender

Ingredients

- Pour 3/4 cup of frozen blueberries into the freezer!
- 3/4 cup of freshly cut strawberries
- 3/4 cup vanilla almond milk, unsweetened, or your preferred milk
- 1 tablespoon peanut butter
- Five to six drops of liquid stevia, or your preferred sweetener
- 1/4 cup of ice
- One scoop of flavorless protein powder, if desired

Instructions

Combine all the ingredients in the blender and blend until a smooth consistency is achieved.

Notes

- Protein: Include a scoop of your preferred unflavored protein powder
- For those looking to enhance their nutrition, consider incorporating a handful of spinach or some frozen cauliflower into your dish. While the taste should remain unaffected, the colour of the spinach may undergo a change.

Nutrition

Serving: 1 smoothie, Calories: 222 kcal, Carbohydrates: 29 g, Protein: 6 g

HOMEMADE CINNAMON APPLESAUCE

PREP TIME 10 MINUTES COOK TIME 20 MINUTES TOTAL TIME 30 MINUTES

Ingredients

- 6 medium apples peeled, cored and quartered
- ½ cup water
- ½ teaspoon ground cinnamon

Instructions

1. Heat all the ingredients in a large pot or Dutch oven over medium-high heat. Let it simmer gently until the apples become tender enough to be easily mashed.
2. With a gentle touch, you can use a masher or even a fork to carefully mash the apples. They should easily break apart without much effort. Blend until it reaches the desired texture. Make sure to chill in the refrigerator before serving.

Nutrition

Serving: 0.5 cup Calories: 117 kcal Carbohydrates: 57.2 protein: 0.7 g

EASY CHIA PUDDING

PREP TIME: 10 MINUTES SOAK TIME: 1 HOUR TOTAL TIME: 1 HOUR 10 MINUTES SERVINGS: 2

Ingredients

- Four teaspoons of chia seeds
- One cup of almond milk

- ½ Tablespoon honey, maple syrup, or preferred sweetener* ¼ teaspoon optional vanilla essence
- Your choice of toppings, such as granola, nut butter, fresh berries, or other fruit

Instructions

1. Combine chia seeds, milk, maple syrup, and vanilla (if desired) in a bowl or Mason jar. If you're using a mason jar, simply seal it tightly and give it a good shake to blend all the ingredients together.
2. After mixing the chia pudding, allow it to rest for 5 minutes. Give it a gentle stir or shake to ensure there are no clumps of chia seeds. Then, cover the mixture and refrigerate it for 1-2 hours or overnight to allow it to set. The chia pudding should have a thick consistency, not too runny. If the consistency is not to your liking, you can simply incorporate some additional chia seeds (approximately 1 tablespoon), give it a good stir, and let it chill in the refrigerator for another 30 minutes or so.
3. Chia pudding can be safely stored for 5-7 days in the refrigerator when kept in an airtight container.

Notes

1. Meal prep: Another option is to prepare your pudding the night before and allow it to chill in the refrigerator overnight for added convenience. Once you're ready to serve, simply add a delightful touch of fresh berries to the pudding and savour every bite.
2. Regarding milk options, I personally prefer almond milk, but any type of milk you have available should suffice. For a light and creamy chia pudding, consider using dairy milk, almond milk, or cashew milk. Using canned coconut milk will result in a luscious and velvety pudding.
3. Reduced sugar option: To create a version with less sugar, you have the choice to omit the sweetener altogether or opt for a sugar substitute such as monk fruit or stevia.
4. Nutrition: Calculating the nutrition facts using unsweetened almond milk and excluding any toppings

Nutrition

Serving: 1serving | Calories: 170kcal | Carbohydrates: 16g | Protein: 7g | Fat: 9g | Sodium: 91mg | Potassium: 96mg | Fiber: 13g | Sugar: 3g

BAKED CINNAMON APPLE CHIPS

PREP TIME: 10 MINS COOK TIME: 2 HOURS TOTAL TIME: 2 HOURS 10 MINUTES

YIELD: 2 CUPS

Ingredients

- 2–4 apples
- Cinnamon, as needed

Instructions

1. Set the oven temperature to 220 F.
2. If you happen to have an apple corer, go ahead and core the apples. If not, feel free to slice them into thin, even rounds using a sharp knife or mandolin slicer, making sure to remove any seeds along the way. For optimal results, aim for thin and evenly sliced pieces when using a knife. To achieve optimal outcomes, it is advisable to ensure that the slices are uniform in size, allowing for even baking.
3. Place the slices in a bowl and generously sprinkle them with a touch of cinnamon. Start with 1/2-1 tsp of the mixture, adjusting as necessary based on the number of apples you used. Mix well and add more if required. Ensure that every apple slice is thoroughly coated by using your hands to mix. If you'd like, you have the option of arranging them on the baking sheet and then sprinkling them with cinnamon. However, I personally prefer mixing them in a bowl to ensure that they are thoroughly and evenly coated on both sides. If you prefer, you have the choice to omit this step and bake them without cinnamon. They are absolutely scrumptious as is!
4. Place the apple slices neatly on a baking sheet lined with a silicone mat or parchment paper.
5. After an hour, take it out of the oven and give it a flip.
6. Continue baking for an additional hour, then switch off the oven and allow them to cool completely inside.

Notes

1. Apples: I enjoy a variety of options, including Gala, Honey crisp, Pink Lady, and Fuji. Granny Smith apples can also be used, resulting in a slightly more tart flavor!
2. Storage: Keep in a sealed container at room temperature for up to 1 week.
3. Spices and Additions: Cinnamon can be a delightful addition if desired. Adding a touch of nutmeg and ginger can also enhance the flavour. To add a touch of indulgence, sprinkle some coconut sugar or powdered sugar along with the cinnamon.

SOFT OATMEAL COOKIES

PREP TIME: 15 MINS COOK TIME: 10 MINS ADDITIONAL TIME: 1 HR 5 MINS

TOTAL TIME:1 HR 30 MINS

Ingredients

- Two cups of all-purpose flour
- 1/2 tsp finely powdered cinnamon
- One tsp baking soda
- One tsp salt and one cup softened unsalted butter
- One cup of powdered sugar
- One cup of dense brown sugar
- Two big eggs
- One tsp vanilla essence
- Three cups of instant oatmeal mixed with flour and nonstick frying spray
- two tsp water
- Two tsp white sugar, or more if necessary

Directions

1. Mix together flour, cinnamon, baking soda, and salt in a medium bowl until thoroughly blended.
2. Mix together butter, 1 cup of white sugar, and brown sugar in a large bowl using an electric mixer until the mixture becomes creamy, which should take around 2 to 3 minutes. Incorporate the eggs, one at a time, and then blend in the vanilla. Blend the dry ingredients into the mixture until thoroughly incorporated. Incorporate the oats into the mixture until they are well mixed. Make sure to cover the bowl and let the dough chill in the refrigerator for at least 1 hour.
3. Before baking, make sure to preheat the oven to 375 degrees F (190 degrees C). Prepare two cookie sheets by spraying them with floured cooking spray. Fill a small bowl with water and another small bowl with 2 tablespoons of sugar.
4. Shape the chilled dough into small balls and arrange them on the cookie sheets, making sure to leave some space between each one. Moisten a big fork in water, then dip it in sugar, and utilize it to gently flatten each cookie, reapplying water and sugar as needed.
5. Cook in the preheated oven until a light golden brown color forms around the edges and the centers are almost set, typically taking 8 to 10 minutes. Remember to switch the racks halfway through for even baking. Let the cookies cool on the baking sheet for 5 minutes before moving them to a wire rack to cool completely.

EASY POACHED PEARS

PREP TIME 20 MINUTES COOK TIME 15 MINUTES TOTAL TIME 35 MINUTES

Equipment

1 Rondeau pan or a large sauce pan

Ingredients

- Water, fruit juice, or wine can fill 750 milliliters.
- 250 milliliters of water
- 200 grams, or less, of granulated sugar, depending on desired level of sweetness
- 1 cinnamon stick or other spices such as whole cloves, star anise, and cardamom seeds, etc.
- One split vanilla bean
- One slice of orange or lemon peel, without pith
- One kilogram of peeled, cored, and chopped pears should weigh 1.8 kg.

Instructions

1. Combine the liquid (whether wine or juice) and water with sugar and spices, vanilla bean, and lemon peel in a large saucepan or sauté pan. Bring the mixture to a boil, gently stirring from time to time with a wooden spoon. Make sure the sugar dissolves completely before moving on to the next steps of the recipe.
2. Place the pears into the simmering poaching liquid and allow it to come to a boil once more. Place a round of parchment on top and use a lid or plate to ensure the pears are fully submerged. Lower the temperature to ensure that the poaching liquid is gently simmering. Cook the pears by gently simmering them for 10 to 15 minutes. The pears should be cooked until they reach a tender consistency without becoming overly soft. It may take up to 45 minutes for the pears to fully cook. One way to determine the doneness of the pears is by using a paring knife. When the pears are cooked to perfection, you should be able to effortlessly pierce through the pear from one end to the other.
3. Drain the pears into a spacious container and allow the poaching liquid to cool down completely. Pour the liquid into the container with the pears, ensuring they are fully covered. Allow the pears to soak and absorb the delicious flavors.
4. As an alternative, straining out the pears and boiling down the syrup will create a delightful accompaniment for the pears.

Notes

1. Opt for red wine to enhance the robustness of the flavour, or choose a light rosé or white for a more subtle taste.
2. Consider substituting maple syrup or honey for granulated sugar to reduce sweetness in the recipe.
3. Feel free to experiment with a variety of sweet and warm spices such as cinnamon, cloves, nutmeg, ginger, star anise, cardamom, and more.

Nutrition

Calories: 305kcal Fiber: 7g Sugar: 48g Vitamin A: 58IU Vitamin C: 10mgCalcium: 33mgIron: 1mg

HEALTHY MANGO YOGURT SMOOTHIE

TOTAL TIME: 5 MINUTES YIELD: 1-2 SERVINGS

Ingredients

- Two cups of frozen mango chunks
- One cup of plain, low-fat yogurt
- A tsp of honey
- One tsp lime juice
- One-half teaspoon of ground cinnamon

Instructions

1. Put all the ingredients in a blender. Puree until velvety and creamy, for approximately one minute.
2. Split the mixture between two glasses or combine it into a single large glass and savor the flavors.

Notes

- For a personalized touch, feel free to experiment with various fruits to create your own unique blend. Just remember to maintain the fruit ratio for a perfectly balanced smoothie. Consider replacing a cup of mango with pineapple or kiwi.
- How to serve: Indulge in this delightful smoothie as is, or get creative by adding some toppings to enhance its flavor and texture. Experiment with different ingredients like granola, shredded coconut, seeds, or fruit.

BAKED APPLE SLICES

PREP: 10MINUTES COOK: 25MINUTES TOTAL: 35MINUTES SERVINGS: 6 SERVINGS

Ingredients

- Two teaspoons of coconut oil or unsalted butter
- Four medium apples, cored and sliced into ¼-inch thick pieces, a combination of tart (like Granny Smith) and sweet-crisp.
- 1/4 cup of pure maple syrup or honey
- One tablespoon of cornflour
- two tsp finely ground cinnamon
- 1/8 teaspoon of ground cinnamon
- 8 grammes of kosher salt
- Two teaspoons of water or bourbon
- Whipped cream or ice cream are optional when serving.

Instructions

1. Set the oven temperature to 350 degrees F.
2. In a generously sized, microwave-safe mixing bowl, warm the butter in the microwave until it becomes liquid. If your bowl is not suitable for the microwave, you can melt the butter in a smaller bowl that is safe for microwaving or in a saucepan on the stove. Afterwards, you can transfer the melted butter into the larger bowl.
3. Add the apple slices, honey, cornstarch, cinnamon, allspice, salt, and bourbon to the mixing bowl. Mix gently to ensure everything is evenly coated.
4. Transfer the mixture into a deep baking dish that measures 9x9 or is of a similar size. Make sure to pour any liquid that has accumulated in the bottom of the bowl over the top.
5. Cook the apples for 25 minutes until they are tender when pierced with a fork but still hold their shape.
6. Enjoy this dish piping hot, and feel free to top it off with a scoop of creamy vanilla ice cream or a dollop of whipped cream, according to your preference.

END

Made in the USA
Monee, IL
04 October 2024